4/03

# A Portrait of Missouri

## 1935–1943

# A Portrait of Missouri

## 1935–1943

## Photographs from the Farm Security Administration

## Paul E. Parker

University of Missouri Press    Columbia and London

Copyright © 2002 by
The Curators of the University of Missouri
University of Missouri Press, Columbia, Missouri 65201
Printed and bound in the United States of America
All rights reserved
5  4  3  2  1    06  05  04  03  02


Library of Congress Cataloging-in-Publication Data

Parker, Paul E.
    A portrait of Missouri, 1935-1943 : photographs from the Farm Security
    Administration / Paul E. Parker.
        p.   cm.
    Includes bibliographical references (p. ) and index.
    ISBN 0-8262-1438-X
    1. Missouri– Social life and customs–20th century–Pictorial works.
    2. Missouri–Pictorial works. 3. Missouri–Rural conditions–Pictorial
    works. 4. Depressions–1929–Missouri–Pictorial works. I. Title.
F466 P265 2002
977.8'042'0222–dc21
                                                                                2002031956


∞™ This paper meets the requirements of the
American National Standard for Permanence of Paper
for Printed Library Materials, Z39.48, 1984.

Jacket Design: Kristie Lee
Text design and composition: Jennifer Cropp
Printing and binding: Thomson-Shore, Inc.
Typefaces: Minion and Bickley Script

*For Michele*

# Contents

# *Acknowledgments*

Especially helpful in seeing this work to completion were the editors at the University of Missouri Press: Clair Willcox for his constructive suggestions and gentle prodding in the development phase, Beverly Jarrett for encouragement in the face of obstacles in getting the prints, and Sara Davis for kind and helpful reading and editing, for persistence in working with the Library of Congress to secure the desired prints, and for guidance through the steps necessary to bring this project to fruition.

Truman State University provided a grant that allowed time for the initial gestation of this project. Colleagues Michele Breault, David Murphy, and Jerold Hirsch contributed much to how I thought about my topic and, thus, how the work developed. Circulation librarian Gayla McHenry and special collections librarian Judy Sapko were exceptionally helpful in facilitating access to needed material. Finally, Greg Brenner and Tom Hayde provided invaluable library research.

*Note to the Reader*

Photographers for the Farm Security Administration kept a record for each photograph, which included a caption as well as the location and date of shooting. The information provided by the photographer, along with the number assigned by the Library of Congress, appears unchanged in the caption for each photo.

*A Portrait of Missouri*

1935–1943

# Chapter 1

*Missouri and the New Deal*

Steele, Missouri. A crowd in front of an itinerant photographer's tent. Russell Lee, August 1938. LC-USF33-011592-M3

"Photos That Looks Like You!" asserts the sign over the tent's entrance. The caption by the government photographer offers some context, telling us where and when this scene was captured. But the story of why the photograph was taken, why the federal government hired photographers and sent them out to make a record of America, and what legacy was left by those photographers sent to Missouri is far more elusive and complex.

To understand why this photograph was made, we must first understand why the federal government employed photographers in the 1930s and 1940s. The Great Depression brought an unprecedented demand by destitute people and their overwhelmed local governments for federal aid to rural America. Relief programs were well received by many farmers, their congressmen, and the governing agricultural bureaus. But some programs went further, aiming to reform American agriculture with new agencies and new practices. Battles were fought over the future organization of farm life and the role that the national government should play in it. One weapon in that battle was publicity: the government hired photographers to create images that would foster positive feelings for its far-reaching plans.

The photographers in the Historical Section of the Resettlement Administration (which later became the Farm Security Administration and eventually folded into the Office of War Information) were hired and directed by Roy Stryker; he decided where they should go and what they should record. Ultimately, the photographers traveled to forty-eight states and took some eighty thousand pictures of life in rural America, capturing far more than just farmers or would-be farmers struggling during hard times. Stryker and those who worked for him were seeking to justify a new agricultural order, but they were also documenting American life. Russell Lee, who shot the itinerant photographer's tent in Steele, was one of at least seven Farm Security Administration (FSA) photographers who visited Missouri (four spent considerable working time in the Show-Me State). Together these seven photographers produced the collection of nearly fifteen hundred pictures upon which this book draws. Fittingly, this chronicle of their work, the programs they sought to promote, and slices of life in Missouri between 1935 and 1943 is a story of politics with its contradictions, tensions, and competing interests.[1]

Photographs, like other stimuli, evoke various responses in people, and responses to the work of the FSA photographers vary across time, political viewpoint, and historical understanding and sympathies. This chapter provides a context for viewing and understanding these images—for reconsidering the people who made them, the people who are depicted in them, the programs they illustrate, and the responses they have elicited. Although the general thrust of the story is well known—dire economic conditions created political demands for greater action by the national government—the demands, and the solutions deemed appropriate to meet them, varied among groups. In the face of these political battles, one agency created to address human need in rural America used photographs to sell its programs. That agency, long since abolished, left a legacy that is now itself a subject of controversy.

## The Depression and Missouri

In the years following the Civil War, political and economic changes reshaped the lives of Americans. The familiar story involves immigration, industrialization, urbanization, and greater centralization of economic and political power. "The central thrust of historical change was to expand, centralize, concentrate, standardize, and institutionalize the external circumstances in which people lived."[2] Notably, the federal government expanded its powers and thus standardized and institutionalized sound economic relations. Congress authorized new agencies to regulate interstate commerce and to oversee new policies in the fields of labor, agriculture, and commerce as well as in the banking industry. But while the expansion of Washington's power could offer benefits to people, it also threatened to take power from local communities, starting a trend that would grow in the 1930s.

By the 1920s, fewer people were employed in agriculture and more in large-scale industry. Henry Ford's automobile assembly line had spread to other industries and reshaped the nature of work, providing for efficiencies that created more consumer goods and higher wages. Still, on the eve of the Great Depression, it appeared that the agriculture sector was rebounding after a postwar slump that had eroded farmers' standard of living. A boom in cotton brought economic and population growth to Missouri's Bootheel, and other parts of the state seemed to be thriving as well: in 1928, 54 million bushels of grain went through the public grain warehouses of Kansas City, and the Missouri Grain Inspection and Weighing Department inspected nearly 86,000 railcars full of grain. That same year, an ambitious statewide road-building plan had received its third boost in a decade, as voters approved $60 million in bonds, and the original goal of building some 7,500 miles of roads had been revised upward. As today, roads were touted as promoting commerce, safety, and convenience, growth from which the farm economy would surely benefit.[3]

Economic booms and busts were known to come and go, but few could predict the depths of the depression of the 1930s or the political revolution it would foment. Missouri, like other states, initially responded with the common palliative of belt-tightening in tough times. In 1931, at the behest of Republican Governor Henry Caufield, the Democratic General Assembly cut state services and the budget. And despite having won handsomely in 1930, Missouri Democrats still played a cautious game in the election year of 1932, with their platform calling for further reductions in state spending and cutbacks in virtually every department.[4]

At the national level, President Herbert Hoover also had been slow to respond to the depression, although by 1932 the federal government had begun offering a couple of loan programs to help keep industry afloat. Additionally, the national government began the massive Hoover Dam project, and it continued to spend hundreds of millions of dollars on federal office buildings. In Missouri, the pace of road building was accelerated, and work on the privately financed Osage

Dam continued. In Kansas City, voter approval of $40 million in bonds for a ten-year building program ensured that construction businesses, including Boss Tom Pendergast's Ready Mixed Concrete plant, would keep running.[5]

While these public works programs supplied jobs for some people, many others were thrown out of work. By 1933, the St. Louis area had lost one-third of its 150,000 industrial employees, and the predepression payroll had been reduced by over one-half. Over the same time frame, the retail trade lost a quarter of its workforce, and wages dropped to half what they had been. Traditionally, relief had been provided by counties, but the conditions of the early 1930s challenged this philosophy of localism. Counties relied upon property taxes, and the average property valuation in Missouri dropped by one-third between 1929 and 1933, precisely while the demand for aid was increasing. In 1932–1933, 39 of Missouri's counties had a tax delinquency rate above 30 percent, and another 43 counties had delinquency rates between 20 and 30 percent. Poor commodities prices and farmers' lack of credit pushed the number of forced sales of farms, bankruptcies, and foreclosures in 1932–1934 to double that of 1925–1929. The counties simply could not meet the demands they faced, and people appealed to a government farther from home.[6]

Three years into the depression, Americans voted for more far-reaching action than belt-tightening and public works projects. In accepting the Democratic nomination for president in 1932, Franklin D. Roosevelt had recognized, "while primary responsibility for relief rests with localities now, as ever, yet the Federal Government has always had and still has a continuing responsibility for the broader public welfare. It will soon fulfill that responsibility." Roosevelt defeated Hoover, and voters also provided FDR with a Democratic Congress that quickly enacted broad legislation. Within a few short months, America would see what FDR's pledge meant in practice. Despite Roosevelt's claims of continuity, by the end of the decade there would be a marked and permanent shift in the roles of local and national governments.[7]

While direct relief was a part of the Roosevelt plan, many programs involved partnerships with the states. For example, Congress authorized the Civilian Conservation Corps (CCC) in April 1933; it provided jobs for young men eighteen to twenty-three years old, some four thousand of whom worked on reforestation, road-building, and construction projects in at least sixteen Missouri state parks. Another program, the Public Works Administration (PWA), required states to raise funds before they could receive relief money from the federal government. After inadequate proceeds from a 1934 occupation tax prevented Missouri from receiving its full share of federal monies, the state adopted a 1 percent sales tax in 1935. Federal dollars flowed into Missouri through this agency and others, including the Federal Emergency Relief Administration (FERA) and the Works Progress Administration (WPA), successor to the PWA. Between 1935 and 1941, the WPA paid $242 million in wages to workers in Missouri. The money helped many people weather the 1930s, while the work performed tangibly benefited the state. Workers built or improved nearly 900 schools and over 750 other buildings, such as courthouses, libraries, and hospitals (nineteen Missouri counties built courthouses with PWA or WPA aid); they laid hundreds of miles of sewer lines, constructed 55,000 bridges and culverts, sewed and distributed over 7.5 million articles of clothing, canned 250,000 quarts of food, and served over 11 million school lunches.[8]

Beyond partnering with the federal government, the state expanded its own role. The State Department of Agriculture was created in 1933, followed by the Department of Conservation in 1936. The state also increased its reach over local governments, assuming more obligations for funding local schools, aiding state and county finances through greater planning, and taking on more responsibility for social welfare (as with passage of an old-age assistance law in 1935). The adoption of the executive budget allowed the legislature to predict revenues and expenditures, and control the spending of agencies. Agency purchasing—from land to electrical services to office supplies—was regularized through a state purchasing agent. Finally, the adoption of a county budget law meant greater planning and oversight of the annual budget process.[9]

These contributions marked a major shift in the roles assumed by the state and federal governments: the New Deal "had expanded substantially the role which the people thenceforth expected government to play in the social and economic life of the states and nation. If the states lost powers to the federal government, which they did, they also gained new ones and, prodded by federal grants-in-aid, accepted new responsibilities, and took over functions previously performed very inefficiently by local units of government."[10]

## The Farmer and Government

While the stock market collapse brought hard times to Wall Street and to many Main Streets, agriculture had been in a precarious position for nearly two decades. The war years had been relatively prosperous for American farmers, but after the war commodities prices fell while costs, including taxes and credit, increased. In

1921, the parity ratio that measured farm income against farm costs was 75, suggesting that farmers' standard of living had fallen by one-quarter since the golden years of 1910 through 1914. Although the economic health of agriculture increased steadily throughout the 1920s, for the decade farmers averaged 85 percent of their prewar income, after accounting for costs.[11]

The congressional response to the farmers' situation was one of several factors that further contributed to the farm difficulties early in the depression. In 1930, Congress passed the Hawley-Smoot Tariff Act, intending to foster higher commodity prices for American farmers by imposing duties on competing imports. However, this protectionist legislation backfired when retaliatory tariffs undermined demand for U.S. exports. If markets shrunk by misguided legislation had been the only challenge farmers faced, perhaps more would have weathered the 1930s, but three other factors wreaked havoc on the farm economy of Missouri and the nation.

First, the banking crisis devastated farmers and small towns whose economies were based on agriculture. Credit has always been important to agriculture in the United States, with farmers often borrowing the money needed to plant by using the potential yield as collateral. Poor yields, or low prices, affect the ability of farmers to repay their loans. One hundred and fifty years before the depression, Massachusetts farmers had rebelled and closed local courts to halt farm foreclosures, an event that precipitated the 1787 Constitutional Convention in Philadelphia. While the Revolutionary War had made it impossible for these colonial farmer-soldiers to pay their debts, in the 1930s, the ravages of the weather and poor markets prevented farmers from earning back their loan amounts when they sold their crops. The overextended banks holding the loans failed, leaving farmers without a source of credit for future plantings.

The weather also caused considerable hardship among farmers throughout the 1930s. The droughts of 1934 and 1936 created the great dust bowl, which prompted hundreds of thousands of people to migrate from Oklahoma and Arkansas in search of work and a better life. And despite the federal government's stepped-up efforts to control rivers through increased channeling and levee construction in the wake of the 1927 flood, the Mississippi and Ohio Rivers flooded in 1933 and 1937. Rarely does a farmer get just the right amount of rain.

The banking crisis, weather, and tariffs all affected farmers' ability to plant, harvest, and sell their crops. A final challenge to their way of life was the culmination of technological and social changes that had been under way for two decades, changes that forced many farmers off the land. One of these changes was the widespread introduction of the tractor. While the large steam tractors of the early twentieth century were more suited to the grain crops of the plains, by the 1930s, tractors with internal combustion engines allowed fewer people to work more acres. In 1930, 900,000 tractors were in use; by 1938, there were 1,500,000. The resultant consolidation of farms promoted agricultural efficiency at the expense of human self-sufficiency. This dislocation of farm families seemed wrong to those who thought, as Thomas Jefferson had, that farm ownership was linked to individualism and agrarian democracy. In 1920, nonowners farmed 41 percent of Missouri farms. These tenancy figures climbed to 49 percent in 1925 and to 54 percent in 1930. Farm tenancy created problems for the people and for the soil. For tenants whose stake in the land was one year's crop, long-term stewardship of the land was secondary to the pressure to pull as much from the soil as possible.[12]

In Missouri, this dislocation was compounded by the changes forced on people who lived along the rivers, especially the Mississippi. Writing in 1913, John Nolen sang the praises of river-drainage programs in southeast Missouri, seeing them as creating a modern-day Eden:

> The Creator seems to have intended these alluvial deposits as a sort of endowment fund, the fruits of which are to be enjoyed after the other soil heritages have been exhausted; they have been held in trust by nature all this time, and defended by the waters. . . .
>
> The reclaiming of this land means that the numerous disease-spreading mosquitoes, lakes, bayous, swamps, "hookworm" and other undesirable objects must give way to wells of pure water, domestic animals, churches, schools, fields of waving grain, orchards, cities and modern dwellings occupied by industrious, frugal, intelligent, contented, happy people.

Largely under the direction of the Little River Drainage District, in "Swampeast Missouri," drainage programs led to the reclamation of nearly two million acres in the seven counties that make up the Bootheel: Butler, Dunklin, Mississippi, New Madrid, Pemiscot, Scott, and Stoddard.[13]

The drainage programs altered local landscape and life both in ways that Nolen anticipated and in some that he did not. The levees and dikes protected rich bottomlands that proved to be well suited to growing cotton, and in the early 1920s when the boll weevil drove cotton out of Tennessee, Arkansas, and Mississippi, the conditions were ripe for the crop's expansion into Missouri. But cotton is hard on both the soil, which it depletes quickly, and on the people who grow it. The changes in southern Missouri—the Bootheel produced over 98 percent of the cotton grown in Missouri—had social and economic consequences that would set the stage for political battles in the 1930s.[14]

While the depression hit all parts of the American economy hard, the factors just discussed created an especially precarious farm economy. Like their urban counterparts, farmers turned to government for assistance. And while the myth of agrarian democracy and self-sufficient individualism is deeply rooted in American culture, in reality the federal government has long played a role as promoter of agriculture. The Homestead Act of 1862 provided for the transfer of public land to people willing to settle on and work claims. Land-grant colleges, and later their extension services, worked with farmers to develop new crop selection, planting, and harvesting techniques. The move from small, self-sufficient farmers selling to local individuals and stores to large operations shipping to national markets was aided by a transportation network promoted through land grants to railroads and the taming of rivers through locks and dams. Additionally, early federal regulations benefited nascent markets. The Interstate Commerce Commission, created in 1887, limited what railroads could charge for the shipping of goods, and the Pure Food and Drug Act of 1908 had created a regulatory framework that, in part, worked to instill faith in products available in the increasingly impersonal marketplace. And now in the face of a hostile environment, farmers, like other Americans, once again sought aid from the national government.[15]

## A New Deal

Roosevelt's new administration wasted no time in creating programs to address the deflated economy and Americans' anxieties. The governmental programs took several different forms, combining what Christiana Campbell refers to as the three r's—relief, recovery, and reform. The three r's, and how to achieve them, were at the center of two political battles regarding national government action: the first, as we have already seen, involved national, as opposed to state or local, action; the second involved the *scope* of the national action, with programs providing relief and recovery meeting with greater acceptance than the more ambitious programs aimed at reforming the farm economy. An additional complication in both struggles was the existence of several classes of farmers.[16]

The relief and recovery efforts were aimed at farmers who theretofore had mostly been successful—people who already owned, or who were buying, land, and who were viewed as having suffered temporary setbacks due to financial and weather conditions that would pass. Essentially, these were good people experiencing bad times. The Emergency Farm Moratorium Act of 1933 allowed many to manage their debts without losing their farms, and the government offered small loans, a program that, especially in light of the banking crisis, met with favor. This monetary aid was readily supplemented by increased technical assistance along the lines of the aid traditionally offered by county extension agents. These promotional relief policies were accepted; however, the unmistakable trend was toward more programmatic control by Washington, which had as advantages the ability to raise revenues (or run deficits) and the distance and resources for long-range planning.

More advanced recovery efforts included rehabilitation programs—"the gradual process of rebuilding both the soil and the people." At their core, these programs aimed to help farmers make wiser choices about land use and crop production, allowing them to be more efficient and productive. The mission of such programs was twofold. First, the programs helped farmers develop efficient cultivating practices that were designed to increase yields and bring higher commodity prices, raising short-term profitability. Second, they encouraged the adoption of farming practices that were more in harmony with the land's productive abilities, thus extending those abilities. Historically, farmers in America have depleted the land and moved on. When there is nowhere left to move, being better stewards of the land takes on more importance.[17]

By contrast, the third "r," reform efforts, promised a more fundamental change. Unlike the relief and recovery programs meant to bridge the submarginal land practices of today and the productive bounties of tomorrow, these programs focused on a portion of the population that had never been in the mainstream of agriculture. As Sidney Baldwin demonstrated in *Poverty and Politics,* his seminal work on 1930s farm policies, Thomas Jefferson's agrarian dream of the democrat-farmer remained a myth not only for the many sharecroppers, who were often only a small step removed from slavery, but also for the increasing number of tenant farmers. However, consistent with our culture of individualism, policymakers and opinion leaders viewed this poverty—the chronic poverty that is passed down through generations, rather than the episodic poverty of a family down on its luck—as a reflection upon the character of the individuals afflicted. Consequently, reform efforts to make farming a dignified living for all farmers, including those farming shares and in tenancy, met with political resistance.[18]

In a tragic bit of irony, the relief and recovery programs not only served different populations than the reform efforts, but those designed to help one group of farmers at times hurt other groups. Among the far-reaching proposals that the Roosevelt administration first brought before the Congress was the Agricultural Adjustment Act of 1933, creating the Agricultural Adjustment Administration (AAA) within the Department of Agriculture. Like the Hawley-Smoot Act three years earlier, a main goal of the AAA was to raise farm prices to the level of the "golden years" of 1910 through 1914. Instead of a tariff, however, the tool would be the restriction of the crop supply. The AAA paid farmers to reduce crop output; decreasing the yield forced prices to increase. But while this accomplished the goal of increasing equality between the agricultural and industrial sectors of the economy, it increased inequality within the agricultural sector. With fewer acres in tillage, landowners needed fewer hired farmers to work the land.[19]

The effects of this policy on the cotton-growing South were especially pronounced, where a single crop required intensive, but seasonal, labor. In the Missouri Bootheel, absentee landowners had large holdings, which were farmed by others. Although AAA guidelines mandated that government payments for reducing crops be split between owners and tenants, many owners discovered they could collect the full AAA payments if they had no tenants on their land. Many tenant farmers were turned off the land, and while they were often rehired as day laborers, they had lost their homes, however ramshackle they might have been. Thus, the success of the AAA's efforts to increase crop prices led to the displacement of sharecroppers and tenant farmers: "as benefit payments for crop reduction increased, the relief load increased in the same counties—clear evidence that the sharecroppers were losing rather than gaining by the program." Government action begat the call for more government action.[20]

## From AAA to RA to FSA

As the depression softened in the mid-1930s, competing philosophies of the role of the federal government clashed. In the eye of the storm, the federal government had been invited to lend a hand. Now, conservatives thought the storm was passing and wanted the federal government to move along as well. On the other hand, reformers welcomed the presence of a strong Uncle Sam and wanted him to stay and do more. In 1935 the reformers won out as Congress enacted a "second New Deal" with programs focused less on temporary relief and more on long-term changes of lifestyle. These agricultural reformers were given the means to effect social change with the creation of the Resettlement Administration (RA), headed by Rexford Tugwell. The RA was largely a consolidation of an "astonishing diversity of projects, programs, and problems" drawn from existing agencies such as the AAA, FERA, and the Subsistence Homesteads Division. As it absorbed other agencies under the ambitious direction of Tugwell, the RA grew from twelve employees to over sixteen thousand in a mere eight months. Its growth and size created both opportunities and political and administrative challenges that would endure for the life of the agency. Created outside the Department of Agriculture, it was freed from control by existing bureaucracies but simultaneously deprived of important allies.[21]

Central programs included land-use planning, resettlement of both urban and rural poor, and a rehabilitation program administered through loans and grants. While the rehabilitation loans and grants were similar to the relief and recovery measures of the AAA, the planning and resettlement programs went much further in changing people's lives and their relations with the government. Tugwell sought to take marginal and submarginal land out of farming and to resettle displaced farmers on sound farmland, when it was available, or in suburban resettlements, when it was not. These latter actions proved to be some of the most ambitious and most contentious undertaken by the federal government.

New Deal programs were consistently ambitious. Roosevelt's brain trust, of which Tugwell was an original member, steadfastly believed that the government could apply the insights of science or social science to fix economic and social problems, and to aid in planning and administration. The creation of the Resettlement Administration, as well as the Rural Electrification Association (REA), and the great engineering undertakings of the Tennessee Valley Authority (TVA) and those responsible for building Hoover Dam, embodied this faith in the federal government's capacities. It was in this context that the Subsistence Homesteads Division built suburban resettlement cities from scratch, including Greenbelt, Maryland, and Greenhills, Ohio. These planned communities offered housing near metropolitan areas without the city crowding. And they were intended to be more than housing: "Greenbelt will be well provided with educational, recreational, social, and shop facilities. Its community center has been designed for maximum use, being so arranged that it has class rooms, gymnasium, and a library. The business center has a market, the management office, a garage, and a variety of stores, as well as a motion picture theater."[22]

Paralleling the suburban subsistence homesteads were the farms of the Resettlement Administration. The federal government purchased land that it then sold or leased to the families selected to participate in the projects; the resettled clients operated the cooperatives. Two of the ninety-nine completed projects were in Missouri: the Southeast Missouri Farms project, which included La Forge Farms, south of Sikeston in New Madrid County, and the Osage Farms project, located near Hughesville in Pettis County.

Political opposition kept the suburban and rural resettlement projects fewer in number and smaller in scale than had earlier been planned. The Resettlement Administration attempted to promote clientele involvement and cast the corporations as examples of the agrarian democracy long hailed as the backbone of America. Consistent with Tugwell's desire to reorganize farming along the model of an industry, one Osage Farms client stated, "This is a corporation, just like any other corporation, except all the stockholders are at work in the corporation at productive enterprises." Despite the idea that the RA was just bringing to agriculture the operational principles that had benefited American industry, the analogy that stuck was one of "Soviet collectivism," trumpeted both in the press and the halls of government. As America emerged from the depths of the depression, the need and desire for more far-reaching reform were lessening.[23]

By late 1937, political reorganization had substantially altered the Resettlement Administration. That year it was renamed the Farm Security Administration, and a director with more modest ambitions and less visibility was appointed. Additionally, the FSA was brought under the authority of the Department of Agriculture, making it more susceptible to such traditional political forces as the American Farm Bureau Federation and the Extension Service. These two established, high-profile interests favored local control over federal reform of agricultural policies.[24]

Having lost its mission for land reform, over the next six years the FSA shifted its attention to helping the small farmer through loans, grants, and agricultural education. By 1943, over 10 percent of American farm families had received an FSA rehabilitation loan; the Farm Credit Administration division is credited with saving 58,000 farms. Cooperative associations, such as grain elevators, were created and promoted; and when military bases were built on the eve of World War II, the resettlement program again played a role in helping families make a new start. By one estimate, in 1940, 50 percent of the farm workers in Missouri's Bootheel were FSA clients. Still there was a lot left undone: of the 146,000 applicants for the Tenant Purchase Program, the FSA could serve fewer than 6,200.[25]

## Picturing the New Role of Government

Almost from the beginning the RA, and its successor, the FSA, had been on the defensive. The agency lacked a clear, well-defined mission. If a central problem was the abundance of people afflicted with poverty, disease, and few hopes, the solution was not obvious. Some saw the goal as getting the tenant farmers onto their own subsistence farms. Others saw this as infeasible: there was not enough decent soil to go around; a government-held mortgage might just present a new set of problems. And all too often, landowners in areas where the FSA was active saw any solution that depleted their source of surplus labor as no solution at all. The different goals of workers at the FSA were reflected in the agency's potpourri of programs, and each one led someone to see the FSA as "The Disturber of the Peace."[26]

Tugwell and his successors zealously defended their programs before Congress, on whom they relied for funding and jurisdictional authority. To sway public, and congressional, opinion the RA/FSA defended and promoted itself through publicity produced by its own Historical Section. Housed within that division was the Photographic Section, under the direction of Roy Stryker. It was not unusual for government agencies to document what they were doing, commonly through congressional testimony or press releases. Nor was the use of photographs unusual: by one estimate 70 percent of federal agencies used pictures during the 1930s. What was unusual was the scope and purpose of the RA/FSA photographs. From 1935 to 1943, Stryker's section amassed some 210,000 negatives and pictures of mostly rural and agrarian life.[27]

While the motivations for creating the FSA photo file were complex, and changed over the course of the project, most directly the aim was to document rural American life and thereby create support for the agricultural reforms pursued by the FSA. The success of the FSA Photographic Section was the result of three factors. First, Stryker used talented photographers: Walker Evans, Dorothea Lange, and Ben Shahn are three of the better-known artists of the twentieth century. Arthur Rothstein, Carl Mydans, John Vachon, and Russell Lee all went on to long, successful careers in photography. This talented ensemble created photographs that were relevant during the depression and repay our attention sixty-five years later. Second, Stryker had a strong sense of how he wanted to use these talented artists. Over his eight-year tenure, he developed a clear vision of what he wanted captured and why; Stryker directed his photographers to make photos that corresponded to shooting scripts based upon this vision. Third, Stryker used his promotional skills to get widespread distribution, and additional publicity, for the photos. Photocollages and stories appeared in newspapers and news magazines; galleries put together shows using images from the FSA files; several contemporary books were produced. As a result of the vision and dedication of Stryker and his photographers, today we have a record of what much of America was like in the 1930s.[28]

The file is more than a collection of photographs documenting a time and place in American history, and photographs are not neutral descriptions of reality. In his invaluable work *Documentary Expression and Thirties America,* William Stott distinguishes between the *document,* an artifact capturing reality, and the *documentary,* which is aimed at motivating through emotions. Stott and others explicitly link the latter with the file. Stryker himself justified this interpretation of the FSA photo project: "In 1936 photography, which theretofore had been mostly a matter of landscapes and snapshots and family portraits, was fast being discovered as a serious tool of communications, a new way for a thoughtful, creative person to make a statement." So the file was intended to influence the emotional state of America, to bolster public support for the New Deal. Indeed, Stryker professed to be "startled—though not displeased—when someone called me 'a press agent for the underprivileged.'" It must be recalled that the scope of the federal government's policies exploded in these few short years, an expansion not met with uniform delight. While we might allow that some of the photographs in the file speak for themselves of the despair and displacement of many Americans, they speak at more of an emotional than an intellectual level. For Stott, this feature is central to an understanding of the file and its importance in American history, politics, and aesthetics.[29]

Just as the motivations for compiling the file were complex, reactions to the photographs and the file are complex. The recognition that the photographs or documents aim to stir our emotions has long been a source of criticism of the file. Rather than a slice of American life, the argument goes, photographers chasing down pictures according to their boss's shooting scripts really assembled a mass of propaganda. Although the label carries disturbing connotations, propaganda need not be any more sinister than "material disseminated by the advocates of a doctrine," a definition that Stryker's actions clearly meet. Sympathizers recognize "it was propaganda in the best sense—that is, the photographs focused attention on real problems and hinted at real solutions." In this light, propaganda is merely informational, with a goal of persuasion. But the term is more commonly used pejoratively, as suggested in the following statement made in the 1930s when public relations efforts by the government were increasing: "Propaganda is to be contrasted with those types of communication that make use of factually accurate and logically adequate explanation." Consistent with this latter view, critical historians argue that the shooting script and the file that it produced represent not typical American life but, in the title of one, the *Symbols of Ideal Life.*[30]

The recognition that photographs are not merely neutral documents but selective re-presentations of the photographer's choosing is further advanced by claims that photographers go beyond *selecting* images to capture and are actively involved in the *posing* of the subjects. Photographer Arthur Rothstein incited a backlash against the FSA by producing multiple shots of a steer's skull against various backgrounds to illustrate a drought in the plains. While this may seem innocuous, a Fargo, North Dakato, newspaper made the photograph an election issue in 1936 by charging that the agency was exaggerating the drought. Instead of focusing attention on real problems, critics charged that the photographers were inventing (or at least misrepresenting) problems. More recently, critics have asserted that families in some of the more famous pictures were posed, including Dorothea Lange's *Migrant Mother,* perhaps the most recognized image in the file. If we are persuaded by such criticism to see the photographs as *fake documents,* the documentary goal of motivating by emotion is undermined by our sense of distrust at being manipulated.[31]

We are left, then, with agreement that Roy Stryker and his photographers were selling something to America. What is disputed is just what they were selling. Seen most benignly, Stryker's program sought to make a case for the basic dignity and worth of human beings, and to persuade Americans that the federal government could address widespread need. They are selling these basic truths. Stryker recognized that the unusual nature of the times allowed the creation of the file. An energetic government seeking to do good things and to develop goodwill was given a few years to try.

But not all persons shared this vision of the good life. Socialists thought the FSA did not go far enough and criticized farm programs like the AAA for helping most those who needed it least. The more conservative Farm Bureau called the work of the RA/FSA too radical, as the governmental policies threatened the tradition of individualism linked to property ownership that the Farm Bureau held to be most clearly represented by traditional American agriculture. More recently, critical historians have argued that the FSA photographic division was emblematic of large institutions—military, corporate, and governmental—aiming to further mainstream liberal ideology of consumer capitalism by selling themselves to obtain legitimacy for their projects.[32]

Thus, the photographic file remains controversial. Competing views of it can most clearly be reconciled by acknowledging that there is complexity, as Stryker did in a series of questions: "Was it sociology?" "Was it journalism?" "Was it history?" "Was it education?" He answered each question affirmatively, although he passed on the question "Was it . . . art?" Surely the photographers were artists, as well as historians and sociologists, educators and advocates. In picking sides in these debates we run the risk of letting labels shape our experience of the photographs—foreclosing other interpretations or viewpoints. Acknowledging this complexity allows us to view the photographs with more understanding.[33]

## One State in the Nation

The photographs taken in Missouri illuminate all of these conflicting roles. Indeed, Missouri's role in the New Deal and the FSA was a complex one. Some FSA administrators had roots in Missouri, as did some of the congressmen and groups working to limit the agency's influence. Notably, the American Farm Bureau Federation, which had origins in and strong ties to Missouri, supported the relief and rehabilitation directed at the traditional middle-class family farm, and at commercial agriculture, but was a powerful critic of the reform needed to address the deeper causes of chronic rural poverty. Other Missouri critics included U.S. House Appropriations Committee chair Clarence Cannon, whom Baldwin identified as one of several committee members "particularly hostile to the FSA."[34]

The photographs selected for this book are intended to illustrate Missouri's complexity and diversity. Even though some fifteen hundred images were taken in the state, not all features of Missouri life are represented. Within the limits of the file's holdings, I have sought to capture the overall experience of life in Missouri in the 1930s. The photographs are organized into six sections. First, there are depictions of the problems that justify government action. These include environmental problems such as erosion and the depletion of marginal farming land, and the photos often show the people attempting to eke out a living in these conditions. Second is a group of photos presenting examples of the more moderate solutions of relief and rehabilitation. These include photos of FSA clients and of extension agents and the better farming and living practices they promoted. A third group reveals the more radical reforms of the FSA, the resettlement of farmers on the Osage and La Forge projects. The establishment and operation of these whole communities was well documented by Russell Lee and Arthur Rothstein. The fourth group documents the famous sharecropper roadside demonstrations of 1939 and their aftermath, which were photographed extensively by Rothstein. Stryker also aimed to capture other aspects of American life in the 1930s, and entertainment, transportation, and social life are prominent themes in the fifth section. The final section shows the transitional nature of the FSA, including the geographic, with photographs of the cities, which served as transportation crossroads for the itinerant photographers, and the temporal—by 1940 Americans were focusing on the military problems of the world, and the photographers, of necessity, did, too.[35]

We have records of photographs in thirty-two Missouri counties, with the vast majority representing southern Missouri, where sharecropping flourished into the 1930s and, thus, where most of the ambitious FSA work was directed. Consequently, these photographs overrepresent the rural lifestyle, but it's a lifestyle that has been important in the history and politics of Missouri and in the history and politics of the federal government, whose photographers made these images. Included are photographs by six of the seven photographers known to have visited Missouri: Russell Lee and Arthur Rothstein contributed the most substantial portion to the file, and to the selections here; the one photograph taken by Marion Post Wolcott in Nodaway County is not included.

# Chapter 2

*Environmental and Human Problems*

Sharecropper family on front porch of cabin, Southeast Missouri Farms. Russell Lee, May 1938. LC-USF33-011529-M1

The FSA photographers produced many images of hardscrabble farms and the people who lived on them in an effort to build popular support for greater national government action. These photographs counter the myth of the self-sufficient agrarian way of life but evoke in some groups an inclination to blame the living conditions on the character, and perceived lack of industry, of the people affected. In the context of the depression, the photos achieved some success portraying larger social forces as a cause of human suffering by showing the impact of an unwelcoming environment.

Part of John Cain family who live in this three-room house near Ashland, Missouri. University of Missouri game and arboretum project. Carl Mydans, May 1936.

LC-USF34-006136-D

Typical dwelling in "Tin Town," Caruthersville, Missouri. Russell Lee, August 1938.

LC-USF33-011590-M2

Sharecropper family
on front porch of
cabin, New Madrid
County, Missouri.
Russell Lee, May 1938.
LC-USF33-011449-M1

Chicken house,
New Madrid County,
Missouri. Russell Lee,
May 1938.
LC-USF33-011510-M2

Eroded land in hilly Ozark farm country, Missouri. John Vachon, May 1940. LC-USF34-061041-D

Pictures like these demonstrate the problem of erosion on logged-over land. By one estimate, thirty-four million acres of once-productive Missouri land had been seriously eroded by 1940, with some areas in the Ozarks losing as much as six inches of topsoil. Viewers could imagine the difficulty of subsisting on worn-out or inappropriate land. Environmental problems are inevitably human problems.[1]

Along with the separate Soil Conservation Service, established within the Department of Agriculture in 1935, the Resettlement Administration/Farm Security Administration was charged with addressing land-use policies through its mission of rehabilitation.

Cotton planted in cut-over field. Mississippi County, Missouri. Carl Mydans, May 1936.
LC-USF34-006242-D

Planting cotton on submarginal farm land along river bottoms. New Madrid County, Missouri. John Vachon, May 1940.
LC-USF34-061066-D

Submarginal cotton farm on the other side of the levee. New Madrid County, Missouri. John Vachon, May 1940.
LC-USF34-061068-D

Twentieth-century artists have employed the plow as a symbol of both good and evil. While the paintings of Grant Wood often celebrate the plow for helping to establish America's breadbasket, fellow painter Alexander Hogue linked a broken plow with erosion and the destruction of Mother Earth. The FSA photographers similarly depicted plows both as tools to aid independence and tools of destruction, most famously in Arthur Rothstein's photograph of a plow on an abandoned dust bowl farm. In this photo in New Madrid County, the plow is prominent, but in this environment it poses a conundrum: how can this land (not) be farmed?[2]

Sharecropper's family at midday meal. Southeast Missouri Farms. Russell Lee, May 1938. LC-USF34-031237-D

While in many pictures families are posed on porches, in this set we get insight into life before modern conveniences like electricity and refrigeration were commonplace. Also, within twenty years, other New Deal programs would make such intergenerational scenes less common. Government-subsidized mortgages would make it easier for young families to purchase homes; Social Security would make it easier for the elderly to keep their homes; and the consolidation of farms would drive more and more youth away from home.

New Madrid County, Missouri. Wife of sharecropper removing fatback from hook in corner of kitchen. Russell Lee, May 1938. LC-USF34-031204-D

"There was little variety in the family's diet of cornbread, fat-back, and molasses, and even in season there was seldom an opportunity for a garden, for the landowner insisted the cotton rows run right up to the cabin."[3]

Wife and child of Ozark farmer, Missouri. John Vachon, May 1940.
LC-USF33-001895-M3

Southeast Missouri Farms. Son of sharecropper combing hair in bedroom of shack. Russell Lee, May 1938.

LC-USF34-031221

Southeast Missouri Farms. Children of sharecropper picking string beans. Russell Lee, May 1938. LC-USF33-011556-M3

Reformers have long favored using children as subjects. Their innocence counters the thesis of the deserving poor.

One government project was building sanitary privies to replace typical sharecropper privies like this one. A survey of 750 Missouri families enrolled in one New Deal farm program revealed that a mere 2.5 percent had indoor bathrooms, and that "unapproved toilets"—those not having a sanitary pit and failing to exclude flies and animals—"were used by 76% of the families."

Posters from the Federal Art Project celebrated improved sanitation conditions, depicting foiled flies unable to spread disease. There were limits to the FSA's ability; modern indoor plumbing was characterized as "coddling" the sharecroppers.[4]

Privy on the premises
of a Negro family before
they moved to a Farm
Security Administration
Delmo group labor
homes house in south-
eastern Missouri. John
Vachon, 1941.

LC-USF34-007640-ZE

Typical windbreak for animals on sharecropper farms, Southeast Missouri Farms. Russell Lee, May 1938. LC-USF33-011527-M2

Sharecroppers and day laborers owned only their labor and were dependent upon a landowner or manager for seed, workstock, and food; tenant farmers stood a rung up on the economic ladder, possessing their own tools and mules. For farmers who could afford them, a team of mules was invaluable for work and transportation.[5]

Working on the levee at Bird's Point, Missouri during the height of the flood. Russell Lee, February 1937.
LC-USF33-011153-M1

After the great flood of 1927, the Army Corps of Engineers built two sets of levees parallel to each other along the Mississippi River in New Madrid County. The land between the levees was to provide a spillway for when the river topped the first levee, or when the Corps purposely sacrificed it, as it did when it dynamited the river levee to open the spillway in 1937. Still, the water rose dangerously high, and people mobilized quickly to sandbag some thirty-five miles of the inland levee.

The flood of 1937 was particularly vicious because it came in the midst of winter. Those who lived in the spillway were forced to evacuate along sleet-covered roads. Bootheel planter Thad Snow believes the hardships endured by the evacuees prepared them and steeled their resolve as roadside demonstrators two years later, in January 1939: they had survived the flood of 1937.[6]

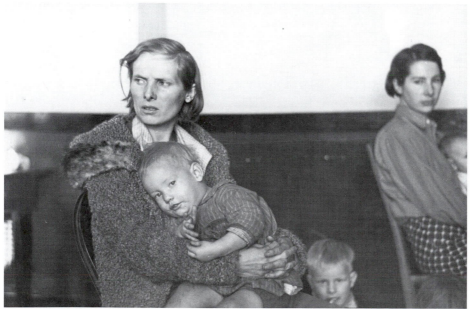

Flooded farm near New Madrid, Missouri. Russell Lee, February 1937.
LC-USF341-010418-B

Mother and child, flood refugees in a schoolhouse at Sikeston, Missouri. Russell Lee, February 1937.
LC-USF33-011159-M1

Mining tiff is a dangerous and laborious occupation because tiff mines are never timbered and all mining is done by hand labor. Washington County, Missouri. Arthur Rothstein, November 1939. LC-USF34-029157-D

Tiff mining in Washington County was the subject of a series of photographs by Arthur Rothstein. With its backbreaking labor that yielded rewards to an absentee landlord while barely providing the laborer with enough to live on, it bore strong parallels to sharecropping. Captions revealed that the tiff (also called barite or white lead) was mined from hand-dug holes ten to fifteen feet deep. A good mine could yield one thousand pounds a day; the tiff sold for six dollars a ton, with about 40 percent going to the landowner and the hauler. Although resettlement projects had fallen out of favor by the late 1930s, there were limited attempts to move tiff miners onto subsistence farmsteads of about fifteen acres each.

Coca-Cola strike, Sikeston, Missouri. John Vachon, May 1940. LC-USF33-001899-M4

Industrial labor also faced challenges in the 1930s. The Wagner Act of 1935 author-ized unions to bargain collectively on behalf of their members, making the strike a legal negotiating tool.

Organized labor doubled its membership in Missouri between 1935 and 1940; part of the growth came from the organization of tiff miners, who went on strike in 1935, and part resulted from the start-up of breweries following the repeal of Prohibition in 1933. With some 250,000 members, the American Federation of Labor (AFL) was stronger in Missouri than in the rest of the nation. Despite these advances, the word-ing of the strikers' sign suggests that social legitimacy still had to be earned.[7]

# Chapter 3

*Relief and Rehabilitation*

Tool shed converted from old log house on Watson homestead. Cuivre River recreational project near Troy, Missouri. Carl Mydans, May 1936. LC-USF34-006120-D

Even the more conservative responses to the problems of the depression, rehabilitation and relief, involved a substantial increase in the power and reach of the federal government. Washington set conditions to be met for receipt of aid, and bureaucrats had the power to give or withhold that aid.

To most farmers and for that matter to most everybody else government on the national level had been a faraway, mysterious thing until 1933. In that year it came right out to our farms and fields, and we welcomed it with open arms. We were ripe and ready for "regimentation." . . . It soon appeared that even banks and other great soulless corporations would gladly surrender their liberties in order to retain life and profits.[1]

One method of softening the reach of the national government was to continue "local control." Federal transfer of land led to the creation of state conservation

Hands of old couple and their granddaughter. Hilly Ozark farm country. Missouri. John Vachon, May 1940.
LC-USF34-061031-D

areas and forests. The Civilian Conservation Corps (CCC), worked on projects such as the Cuivre River Federal Recreation Demonstration Area and aided in the creation of the University of Missouri Game Arboretum near Ashland. Cuivre River State Park was formed in 1946 when the federal government transferred the land to the state.[2]

A photograph of hands? Taking seriously Roy Stryker's declaration that his photographers respected the dignity of their subjects, we might interpret the photograph above as a tribute to multiple generations or as a basic prophecy. A similar photograph in the file has been criticized for affronting the dignity of a subject by reducing her to her hands.[3]

Background photo, family of Negro FSA (Farm Security Administration) client, who will participate in tenant purchase program. Caruthersville, Missouri. Russell Lee, August 1938.

LC-USF33-011598-M2

Family of FSA (Farm Security Administration) client, former sharecropper, on porch of old shack home. New Madrid County, Missouri. Russell Lee, May 1938.

LC-USF33-011490-M5

Background photo. FSA (Farm Security Administration) client who will become owner-operator under tenant purchase program, Caruthersville, Missouri. Russell Lee, August 1938. LC-USF33-011602-M3

FSA (Farm Security Administration) client with three sons, Caruthersville, Missouri. Russell Lee, August 1938.
LC-USF33-011602-M5

Two pictures, selected from several of the same Caruthersville family, show the role the photographer could play in posing the family to influence our emotions and evaluations. The photo on the previous page appears to show seven members of the family in a moment of relaxation. The eye is kept busy, not only with the family members, but also with features in the background, such as the hanging overshirts, the child in the window, and another figure nearly hidden in shadow. Questions about relationships go unanswered. In the second, more direct photograph, above, a man and his sons stand tall and proud. The photographer has removed the clutter of the first photo (including women), and shifted the location a few feet to the right. This frames the subjects between the porch posts and eliminates the distraction of the window in the background. The dirt in the foreground has been cropped, and the left side easily could be trimmed, making this a much cleaner, more powerful photo. The first photo invites questions about the living habits of the family; the second demonstrates that aiding the man (an FSA client) will aid future generations.

Family of sharecropper on front porch, Southeast Missouri Farms. Russell Lee, May 1938.
LC-USF33-011445-M4

While the previous images can be read as examples of the government photographer trying to shape impressions, there is evidence that the subjects themselves engaged in impression management, as well. The people in the photo above are dressed in their finest. The extra fabric required for the double-breasted, pleated dresses is a sign of surplus, and the men sport felt hats, rather than the cheaper and more utilitarian straw hats.[4]

FSA (Farm Security Administration) client with mules bought by government loan, Southeast Missouri Farms. Russell Lee, May 1938. LC-USF33-011568-M5

Rehabilitation Administration supervisor Keller pointing to calves born from cows purchased with rehabilitation loan to Mr. Wilks. Callaway County, Missouri. Carl Mydans, May 1936. LC-USF34-006154-D

Relief and rehabilitation included helping farmers become more self-sufficient through the purchase of equipment, livestock, and seed. The presence of the rehabilitation supervisor in the photo above suggests the regimentation spoken of in the quotation at the beginning of this chapter.

While photographs from the early years often focused on the abject poverty of "the bottom third," the approach of Stryker and his photographers evolved; by 1938 they were also taking more positive photographs.[5]

Southeast Missouri Farms. Wife of FSA (Farm Security Administration) client feeding chickens. Russell Lee, May 1938.
LC-USF33-011531-M2

Farm workers in Southeastern Missouri augmenting their sparse income by growing their own food in a spring garden (Labor Rehabilitation Program). Dryden, between 1935 and 1942. LC-USF34-014187-D

Southeast Missouri Farms. FSA (Farm Security Administration) clients preparing greens for canning. Russell Lee, May 1938.

LC-USF33-011466-M4

Drying jars at canning time. A house purchased for the Lake of the Ozarks project. Missouri. Carl Mydans, May 1936.

LC-USF34-006221-D

Each family cans a large portion of its food raised in its own garden. Osage Farms, Missouri. Arthur Rothstein, November 1939. LC-USF34-029075-D

Workers in the field of home economics taught clients how to make their households more efficient, productive, and healthy. The FSA drew on the success of such programs and distributed pressure cookers. FSA clients were encouraged to put up seventy-five to eighty quarts of fruits and vegetables for each household member. By one estimate, the canning of food for home consumption tripled in three years. This group of photos (opposite, above, and over) clearly show the results of the housewives' labors and demonstrate some of the opportunity for social interaction this life provided in the decades before double-income families, frozen dinners, and drive-throughs.[6]

Mrs. Dixon cans an adequate supply of fruits and vegetables to give her family a balanced diet during the winter. St. Charles County, Missouri. Arthur Rothstein, November 1939. LC-USF34-029145-D

Bates County relocation project, Missouri. Mrs. Fred Whitesell who moved with the aid of FSA (Farm Security Administration) after their land in Newton County, Missouri was bought by the army for construction of Camp Crowder. John Vachon, February 1942. LC-USF34-064337-D

A series of positive propaganda photos depicted the Dixon family of St. Charles County. Captions on several of the photographs tell a story of the FSA's role:

"The Dixon family planning their farm program. Since becoming rehabilitation clients, they have changed from wheat farming to livestock raising."

"The FSA county home supervisor is helping Mrs. Dixon to plan a practiced way of managing her household."

"The health of the Dixon family is taken care of by the medical cooperative established by the FSA."

Since becoming reha-
bilitation clients the
value of the Dixon
family's possessions
has risen from 500
dollars to 1500
dollars. St. Charles
County, Missouri.
Arthur Rothstein,
November 1939.

LC-USF34-029143-D

Oran, Missouri. Doctor's office and waiting room. John Vachon, February 1942. LC-USF34-064353-D

Opposite, we see a well-lit portrayal of literacy and leisure. The oil lamp and a strong shadow cast by Mr. Dixon's head, likely from the photographer's lighting, betray the staging of the photo.

Government programs also included medical and dental care; according to a contemporary report, "when [FSA] loan failures were analyzed . . . it was found that about half were caused by bad health." Some 80,000 families, or 400,000 people, were enrolled in FSA-organized plans and paid a monthly fee into a pool from which a panel paid service claims filed by physicians and hospitals who participated in the program. Such "group health care" was another point of contention on the collectivism that the government was pushing.[7]

Dunklin County, Missouri. Farm boy using welding equipment on a farm that receives U.S. Rural Electrification Administration (REA) power. Arthur Rothstein, July 1942. LC-USW3-006682-D

Often attacked for its ambitious programs, the FSA attempted to make allies of other agencies. FSA photographs were known to be of high quality and were made available to the press and to government agencies free of charge. Above is a publicity shot for the REA. To develop support, the REA had to convince many Americans that electric power was both safe and useful.[8]

During the 1937 flood, most of the Resettlement Administration was turned over to the Red Cross, who made it their headquarters. Russell Lee, January 1937. LC-USF34-010470-D

The Washington bureaucracy of the Resettlement Administration had the political acuity to share its headquarters with the Red Cross during the flood of 1937. In the photo above, posters on the wall reflect the RA's mission, while the photo of the RA office occupying a former grocery store (over) demonstrates the integration of the RA into the community.

During the 1937 flood, most of the Resettlement Administration office in Sikeston, Missouri, was turned over to the Red Cross as headquarters for their relief activities in southeastern Missouri. Russell Lee, January 1937.
LC-USF341-010417-B.

# Chapter 4

*Radical Reform: Resettlement*

House plant. General view precutting operation. Material in this picture moves from background to foreground. Southeast Missouri Farms project. Russell Lee, May 1938. LC-USF33-011494-M2

Among the more ambitious farm programs was that which gave the Resettlement Administration its name. The government purchased land and built houses for thousands of families. In the photo above, an overview of a housing assembly plant illustrates the planning and efficiency that were the hallmarks of the faith of the reformers.

House plant. Precutting materials. Southeast Missouri Farms Project. Russell Lee, May 1938.
LC-USF33-011573-M3

In addition to housing, the projects provided regular jobs for skilled and unskilled laborers. Russell Lee's photograph of the saw guard in this photo likely goes beyond serendipity. The photographers took hundreds of pictures in a week and were often attuned to nuances that would tell a story. Here the saw guard protects the worker, while the "Rex" label hints at royalty, signifying for the viewer the dignity FSA photographers sought to capture.[1]

Housing plant. Moving completely assembled panel to stacks. Southeast Missouri Farms Project. Russell Lee, May 1938.
LC-USF33-011484-M5

Barn erection, raising panel to sill, Southeast Missouri Farms Project. Russell Lee, May 1938.
LC-USF33-011569-M1

Southeast Missouri Farms Project. House erection. Interior view of gable end after erection. Note 2" x 6" bottom plate of gable end which provides nailing for ceiling boards of the interior finish. Russell Lee, May 1938.

LC-USF33-011500-M5

Southeast Missouri Farms. Family of FSA (Farm Security Administration) client, former tenant farmer, on front porch of new home. Russell Lee, May 1938. LC-USF33-011462-M3

An "after" shot (above) depicts a family on the porch of their new house, on its way to becoming their home. An obviously staged photo (opposite) may strike the viewer oddly, but the construction of sanitary privies was a major FSA goal.

One of the scattered labor homes with privy. New Madrid County, Missouri. John Vachon, November 1940.
LC-USF34-061847-D

Captions from the many photos of the government-constructed homes describe them in simple terms: buildings with four or five rooms, costing $500 to $700, although a press report at the time estimated costs at $930 to $1,105, "including overhead." Wiring, built-in cabinets, hardboard walls, and ceilings distinguished them from the cabins they typically replaced. Generally, the chosen family was expected to pay the low-interest mortgage over a period of thirty to forty years.[2]

Southeast Missouri
Farms. Wife of client
in kitchen of new
home. La Forge
project, Missouri.
Russell Lee, May
1938.

LC-USF34-031152-D

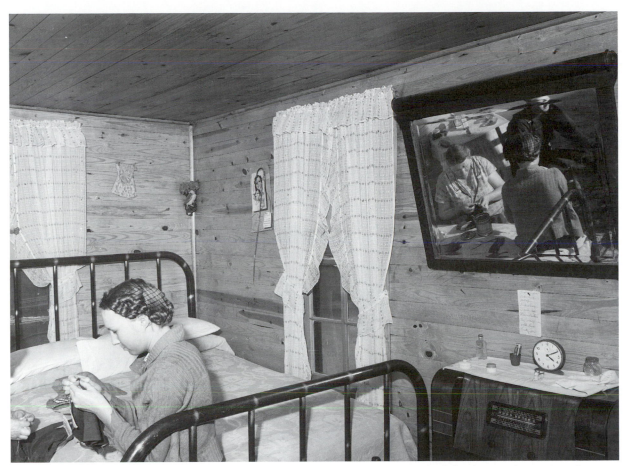

Combination living and bedroom in one of the four-room scattered labor homes built by the FSA (Farm Security Administration) at a cost of five hundred dollars. New Madrid County, Missouri. John Vachon, May 1940.

LC-USF34-061866-D

Initially, the resettlement projects focused on building entire communities on government-purchased land. After the sharecropper strike of 1939, the increased need for housing was partially met through the building of "scattered," or "infiltrated," homes. These new projects were smaller and mixed with non-FSA homes, making communal efforts and organization more difficult.

Southeast Missouri Farms. Customers examining stock of cooperative store. La Forge project, Missouri. Russell Lee, May 1938. LC-USF34-031111-D

The La Forge Farms project, opened in 1937 in southeast Missouri, developed wholesale communities, including homes, schools, community centers, and a store, and resettled one hundred families on six thousand acres. The picture of the store's interior on opening day is a traditional documentary photograph, showing stocks of goods, an integrated clientele, and the simple construction that can later accommodate a stove. The next photograph can be read on two levels: shown are commercial goods available locally for purchase, but the photographer's inclusion of the "Safety-Ray" product suggests the comfort and protection that La Forge Farms provides the resettled clients.[3]

Display of goods in store, La Forge, Missouri. Russell Lee, May 1938.
LC-USF33-011584-M5

Negro school. Southeast Missouri Farms. Arthur Rothstein, January 1939.
LC-USF34-026879-D

White schoolroom near Southeast Missouri Farms. Russell Lee, August 1938. LC-USF34-031305-D

Tug-of-war at school, Southeast Missouri Farms Project. Russell Lee, August 1938. LC-USF33-011605-M2

The farm resettlements were meant to be communities, where people worked and learned and played. Photos of the Negro school at Southeast Missouri Farms show a sturdy, handsome building, beyond the reach of sharecroppers. In the photo above, playing tug-of-war, are healthy, happy children. And, of course, the photos together show the limits of the FSA projects. Locally, the integration of La Forge Farms was seen as more evidence that Washington bureaucrats and the "book farmers," as the extension agents were sometimes called, did not understand what they were doing. Subsequent programs, already on precarious political footing for taking on traditional agriculture, did not challenge segregation.

Group of homes located near the dairy farms on Bois d'Arc Cooperative farm. The same well and pump that furnishes water for the barns serves to supply the homes. Osage Farms, Missouri. Arthur Rothstein, November 1939.

LC-USF34-029015-D

In addition to the Southeast Missouri Farms project, the FSA created two sets of cooperative farms in Pettis County, north of Sedalia. The Bois d'Arc Cooperative and the Hillview Cooperative together made up Osage Farms. One caption from 1939 reads, "The Bois d'Arc cooperative supports twenty-one families on its 1885 acres. The Hillview cooperative supports eight families on its 596 acres. The thirty-six individual units have from seventy to eighty acres."

Compared with those of Southeast Missouri Farms, these photos show more substantial homes and buildings. For the few years that the cooperatives lasted, the

Buildings are efficiently designed for modern farm methods. Bois d'Arc Cooperative. Osage Farms, Missouri. Arthur Rothstein, November 1939. LC-USF34-029012-D

main farming was done in common, with shares, but, as the captions point out, each family had its own garden plot. Another caption declared, "Feed rations for hogs are scientifically determined." These experiments in collective farming were promoted as democratic communities but criticized as communistic.

The collective nature of the farms allowed farmers to share expensive equipment they otherwise could not have afforded, but that equipment would soon contribute to the surplus of farm labor, as fewer people could handle more acreage.

Large scale farming with tractors means greater profits on the Bois d'Arc cooperative. Osage Farms, Missouri. Arthur Rothstein, November 1939. LC-USF34-028903-D

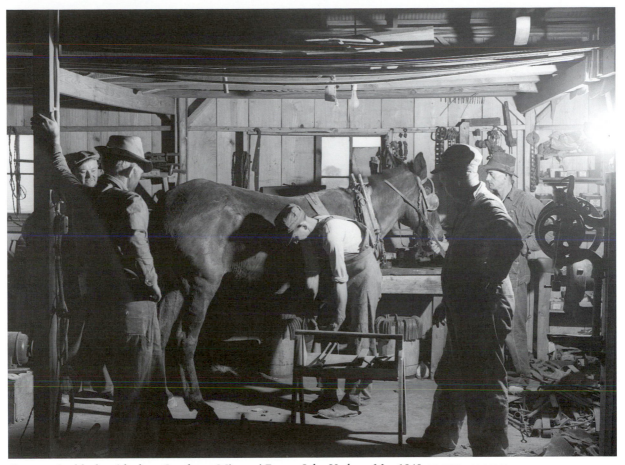

Cooperative blacksmith shop. Southeast Missouri Farms. John Vachon, May 1940. LC-USF34-061038-D

The positive propaganda photographs on the following pages depict FSA successes: strong, clean, healthy clients and their children.

Member of Hill-view cooperative who formerly lived in submarginal farm area. Osage Farms, Missouri. Arthur Rothstein, November 1939.
LC-USF34-028911-D

Wife and child of member of Hillview Cooperative. Osage Farms, Missouri. Arthur Rothstein, November 1939.
LC-USF34-028917-D

Members of the Bois d'Arc Cooperative looking over their accounts. Osage Farms, Missouri. Arthur Rothstein, October 1939. LC-USF34-029006-D

Organized meetings provided clientele the opportunity to have a hand in directing the affairs of the farms, consistent with their democratic nature. An article about the Hillview Cooperative in the 1938 *Kansas City Star* strongly emphasized this aspect of the farms, quoting members who likened the farm to a corporation managed for the good of the shareholders. This new, democratic approach to cooperative farming was seen as too radical by established interests. In 1943 Congress ordered the FSA to liquidate its holdings. In most cases, this meant the division of the cooperative farms into sections to be held by a few owners. The scattered homes of southeast Missouri were bought by the Delmo Corporation, from St. Louis, which then carried the notes so the families could realize their goal of homeownership.[4]

Meeting of farmers and wives to discuss farm problems. Southeast Missouri Farms. John Vachon, May 1940.
LC-USF34-061008-D

Negro clients, Southeast Missouri Farms. Meeting at project. Russell Lee, August 1938. LC-USF33-011585-M1

# Chapter 5

*Sharecropping: The Stubborn Problem*

New Madrid County, Missouri. Sharecropper's wife chopping cotton, Southeast Missouri Farms Project. Russell Lee, May 1938. LC-USF33-011545-M3

Sharecropping came relatively late to Missouri. The Bootheel was transformed over a few short years in the mid-1920s by the arrival of cotton, made possible by drainage projects and made necessary by the boll weevil in states further south. An influx of mostly black sharecroppers—by one estimate, ten thousand in two months of 1924 alone—followed the cotton. Large landowner and planter Thad Snow declared it an "astounding metamorphosis . . . the cotton South moved up and absorbed us."[1]

New Madrid County, Missouri. Sharecropper cultivating cotton. Southeast Missouri Farms. Russell Lee, May 1938.
LC-USF33-011541-M2

Negro cotton worker, New Madrid County, Missouri. Russell Lee, May 1938. LC-USF33-011534-M2

In 1939 the budget of the FSA was $175 million. Programs like "land rehabilitation" are abstract, and such budgets can dwarf our comprehension. But programs and budgets serve people, and the FSA Photographic Section aimed to show the face of rural poverty to the American people. These photos (above and opposite) of women sharecroppers capture the human dignity that was important to Stryker as well as the uncertainty that marked their lives.

Sharecropper's wife with hoe. New Madrid County, Missouri. Russell Lee, May 1938. LC-USF33-011554-M5

Evicted sharecroppers along Highway 60, New Madrid County, Missouri. Arthur Rothstein, January 1939.
LC-USF33-002927-M4

Of course, not all of the programs succeeded. Under the Agricultural Adjustment Act, farmers were paid to reduce the land in production. Landowners, desiring not to share the government payments, kicked the tenants off the land. Led by Reverend Owen Whitfield, a member of La Forge Farms, evicted tenant farmers set up camps along Highways 60 and 61 in southern Missouri to draw national attention to the fact that, nearly ten years after the start of the depression, economic hardship had not been addressed in all places and for all people.[2]

Evicted sharecroppers along Highway 60, New Madrid County, Missouri. Arthur Rothstein, January 1939.
LC-USF33-002926-M3

Arthur Rothstein captured numerous images of the tenants' strike. Some provide perspective—the barren winter fields, the long lines of tenants with their worldly possessions protected only by tarps, if at all—and some, as above and on the following pages, show the humanity.

Evicted sharecropper and child, New Madrid County, Missouri. Arthur Rothstein, January 1939.

LC-USF33-002945-M2

Evicted sharecroppers along Highway 60, New Madrid County, Missouri. Arthur Rothstein, January 1939.
LC-USF33-002929-M3

Evicted sharecroppers along Highway 60, New Madrid County, Missouri. Arthur Rothstein, January 1939.
LC-USF33-002919-M3

Evicted sharecroppers along Highway 60, New Madrid County, Missouri. Arthur Rothstein, January 1939.

LC-USF33-002924-M2

Evicted sharecropper, New Madrid County, Missouri. Arthur Rothstein, January 1939.

LC-USF33-002921-M3

Wife of evicted
sharecropper, New
Madrid County,
Missouri. Arthur
Rothstein, January
1939.
LC-USF33-002967-M5

Evicted sharecroppers along Highway 60, New Madrid County, Missouri. Arthur Rothstein, January 1939.

LC-USF33-002943-M3

State highway officials moving sharecroppers away from roadside to area between the levee and the Mississippi River, New Madrid County, Missouri. Arthur Rothstein, January 1939. LC-USF33-002932-M3

The strike, which began on Monday, January 9, 1939, brought unwanted national attention to southeast Missouri. The landowners and planters, afraid of bad publicity or an investigation that would show they had displaced farmers in order to collect greater government payments, attempted to discredit the strikers. Critics of the protesters suggested that outside agitators and communists had instigated this un-American action; such charges would be made two decades later by people attempting to discredit the civil rights movement. Both actions were guided by religious leaders, who risked their own safety.[3]

Governor Stark instructed the state to work with the Red Cross in providing assistance, but the Red Cross refused to aid the strikers, declaring that they had placed themselves in the situation. Promises of state aid were made, but action was delayed,

State highway officials moving evicted sharecroppers away from roadside to area between the levee and the Mississippi River, New Madrid County, Missouri. Arthur Rothstein, January 1939. LC-USF33-002932-M2

and red tape prevented much local aid from being rendered. The state health commissioner conducted a cursory inspection of the camps on Thursday and ordered them broken up, reversing his earlier statement that the camp posed little threat to health. The state police began to remove protesters on the fifth day of the strike.[4]

New Madrid County, Missouri. State highway officials moving sharecroppers away from roadside to area between the levee and the Mississippi River. Arthur Rothstein, January 1939. LC-USF33-002975-M2

The photograph above is one of several by Rothstein that includes road signs. Once again, we see a photograph that works on more than one level. Most simply, it documents the location of an event: Highway 60 at the junction of county roads H and N. The road signs also serve as a metaphor. The farmers are at a crossroads in their lives and in American history. Sharecropping is waning as an institution. The arrows indicate directions for the future, but the photos make clear that these people have little to sustain them beyond their determination and solidarity.

Photographer Arthur Rothstein revisited the strike area ten months later, in November 1939. Some families had been taken back onto "their" land, and a rejuvenated FSA resettlement program held the promise of opportunities for others in the Delmo, Grayridge, and Morehouse group labor homes of Southeast Missouri Farms. A third group had been moved to some ninety acres of land purchased by a group from St. Louis. Unlike most government resettlement communities, this community, Cropperville, was racially integrated, although segregated by life chances.

Sharecroppers being moved from highway to area between levee and the Mississippi River, New Madrid County, Missouri. Arthur Rothstein, January 1939.
LC-USF33-002929-M1

New Madrid spillway where evicted sharecroppers were moved from highway, New Madrid County, Missouri. Arthur Rothstein, January 1939.
LC-USF33-002918-M1

Evicted share-
cropper building
a cabin. Butler
County, Missouri.
Arthur Rothstein,
November 1939.
LC-USF34-029211-D

Cabins built by evicted sharecroppers. Butler County, Missouri. Arthur Rothstein, November 1939.
LC-USF34-029179-D

Cropperville operated for a decade with the help of the St. Louis relief group and continued on into the 1960s after the group's withdrawal. At least two people were still living on the Cropperville land as late as 1992.

State pressure on planters to let sharecroppers stay on the land ended renewed threats of roadside strikes in 1940. While the sharecroppers' strike provided the impetus for expanding the FSA's resettlement program in southeast Missouri, time was running out. War restrictions on building had halted construction of FSA communities by 1942, as America turned its attention overseas.[5]

Washing clothes at camp for evicted sharecroppers. Butler County, Missouri. Arthur Rothstein, November 1939.
LC-USF34-029196-D

# Chapter 6

*A Broader Slice of Missouri Life*

Peculiar, Mo., Population 206. John Vachon, January 1942. LC-USF33-016197-M2

The photographers' travels took them through much of Missouri; photographs exist from nearly one-third of the state's 114 counties. Stryker instructed all the FSA photographers to go well beyond the farm problems and the government-offered solutions. Perhaps best known are Walker Evans's photographs of the South, which capture folkways and life. But the file as a whole preserved for later generations aspects of American life in the 1930s. This grouping offers us glimpses of modes of transportation, entertainment, and social life.

Nevada, Missouri. In front of the courthouse. John Vachon, February 1942. LC-USF34-064322-D.

A trip to town on Saturday afternoon offered opportunities for economic and social exchange. Above, the Nevada square in 1942, complete with a hitching rail. In the following picture of Steele, the subjects' fine dress reveals the significance of the occasion.

Negro women in front of ten cent store, Steele, Missouri. Russell Lee, August 1938.

LC-USF33-011596-M4

Negro delivery boy, Caruthersville, Missouri. Russell Lee, August 1938.

LC-USF33-011600-M1

Spectators at cattle
auction, Sikeston,
Missouri. Russell
Lee, May 1938.
LC-USF33-01155-M1

Farmers at auction sale, Sikeston, Missouri. Russell Lee, May 1938. LC-USF33-011515-M5

Depression-era foreclosures were an impetus for greater national government involvement, including the farm programs. Most of these foreclosures happened before the Resettlement Administration was created in 1935 (and, thus, before photographers were sent forth). Here, the photographs of livestock and farm auctions offer a more benign social and economic picture.

Horse is paraded before prospective buyers, farm sale, Pettis County, Missouri. Arthur Rothstein. November 1939.

LC-USF-33-003449-M2

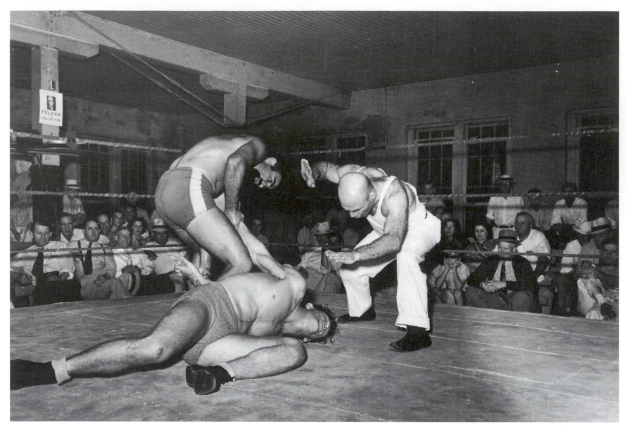

A wrestling match sponsored by American Legion, Sikeston, Missouri. Russell Lee, May 1938. LC-USF33-011526-M2

Stryker's vision of the file included photographs of ordinary people doing ordinary things. On a 1938 trip to Sikeston, Missouri, Russell Lee captured a social life that preceded air-conditioning and television.

In addition to illustrating social life in the early 1940s, pictures of events such as a picnic during the Hayti Cotton Festival (opposite) served to show a more prosperous and healthy America, an America that would be able to defend her interests in a world full of turmoil.

Hayti, Missouri. Cotton carnival. Picnic. Arthur Rothstein, July 1942.

LC-USW3-006603-D

Magazines at newsstand,
St. Louis, Missouri. Arthur
Rothstein, January 1939.
LC-USF33-003025-M5

Children looking at posters in front of movie. Saturday, Steele, Missouri. Russell Lee, August 1938. LC-USF33-011594-M1

Other forms of entertainment–a newsstand in St. Louis, the movie house in Sikeston, and a traveling minstrel show–offered escapism and the promise of romance.

Here (page following) is the small Lake of the Ozarks community following the completion of the Osage Dam in 1931. To clear space for the reservoir created by the dam, people from five communities were relocated. An increased standard of living and improved highways over the next several decades remade this previously isolated area into the state's major recreation destination. Increased automobile travel meant that tourist facilities had to compete for traffic; thus, a tourist camp in Shannon County offers an eye-catching exterior.

Carnival employee
sleeping in hammock
underneath wagon.
Lasses-White show.
Sikeston, Missouri.
Russell Lee, May
1938.
LC-USF34-031272-D

View of Lake of
Ozarks settlement.
Missouri. Carl
Mydans, May 1936.
LC-USF34-006165-D

Shannon County, Missouri. Gas station and tourist cabins. John Vachon, February 1942. LC-USF34-064299-D

Half-way bus station between Memphis and St. Louis, New Madrid, Missouri. Russell Lee, May 1938.
LC-USF33-011571-M3

Ferry to Tennessee from New Madrid County, Missouri. Russell Lee, May 1938. LC-USF33-011580-M3

Small ferries allowed travelers to cross rivers when bridges were uncommon; today, five ferries still provide service across the Mississippi River to Illinois and Kentucky.

Dunklin County, Missouri. Children in a consolidated rural school. Arthur Rothstein, July 1942.
LC-USW3-006693-D

The populations (and tax bases) of many rural communities continued to decline, while curriculum demands increased. The movement toward consolidated schools accelerated in the 1930s.

Newton County, Missouri. Camp Crowder area. Signs along U.S. Highway No. 71. John Vachon, February 1942.
LC-USF34-064279-D

The wry humor of photographer John Vachon is expressed in this juxtaposition of signs offering competing spirits.

In the following photo the "social documentary is more disturbing," as the caption makes clear. Throughout history, a companion to change has been resistance to change, commonly in the form of intimidation and violence. Race relations traditionally had been left to state and local governments to handle, but with the expansion of the national government's power, civil rights gradually moved onto the national agenda, although congressional opponents of civil rights continued to defeat antilynching legislation in the 1930s and 1940s. A photograph showing a black man voting is valuable propaganda; segregation at home undermined our moral authority to wage war again totalitarian regimes.[1]

New Madrid County, Missouri. The "Hanging Tree." Several Negroes have been hanged on this tree. Russell Lee, May 1938.
LC-USF34-031245-D

Dunklin County, Missouri. Voting in the primary election at the county courthouse. Arthur Rothstein, July 1942.
LC-USW3-006633-D

Mules. Chillicothe, Missouri (vicinity). John Vachon, February 1942. LC-USF34-064247-D

The mule rightfully holds a special place in Missouri lore. Before the arrival of the tractor, pioneers and farmers owed their ability to clear and work land to the strong, determined animal. Bootheel planter Thad Snow, for instance, devotes a chapter of his memoirs to recollections of a particularly fine mule, Kate.

Among the more famous FSA photographers is Dorothea Lange. In 1938 she visited southeast Missouri briefly and produced a series of photographs of a family heading home from town on a Saturday evening.

Southeast Missouri. Horse and wagon is still a common means of transportation. Dorothea Lange, August 1938.
LC-USF34-018981-E

# Chapter 7

*The Cities and the Coming War*

Thomas Jefferson statue in front of state capitol. Jefferson City, Missouri. John Vachon, May 1940.
LC-USF34-060954-D

Railroad station, Jefferson City, Missouri. John Vachon, May 1940. LC-USF33-001903-M5

   While the main mission of the FSA photographers was to document the struggles of rural, specifically farm, life and the government programs that addressed them, Stryker envisioned a broader collection of images of American life, which included photographs of urban areas. These were easily gathered, as cities provided the transportation hubs through which the photographers often had to travel to reach their more rural destinations. In the selections that follow we see some of these urban photographs, and we also see the changing nature of the FSA. As it became clear that America would be drawn into World World II, it was obvious that a collection of photos depicting a destitute and downtrodden America would afford propaganda of the wrong kind to the enemies of American strength and security.

   The RA/FSA itself was changing; relief and rehabilitation had aided many in the farm sector through the worst years of depression, but now the coming war both created greater demands for American harvests and offered employment to many who had left farming.

Mississippi River steamers. St. Louis, Missouri. Arthur Rothstein, March 1936. LC-USF34-001835-E

Modern riverboat, St. Louis, Missouri. John Vachon, May 1940. LC-USF33-001879-M1

Arthur Rothstein made trips to St. Louis in 1936 and 1939, and John Vachon visited in 1940. In their photos, we are offered clear parallels between rural and urban America. Both were evolving: as the horse and buggy existed alongside the automobile, the stern-wheeler existed alongside the modern and streamlined *Admiral.* And poverty affected urban as well as rural areas.

Mailboxes for squat-
ters along the river,
St. Louis, Missouri.
Arthur Rothstein,
January 1939.
LC-USF33-002989-M2


Children's playground.
St. Louis, Missouri.
Arthur Rothstein,
March 1936.
LC-USF34-001840-E

Work Projects Administration riverfront improvement project, St. Louis, Missouri. Arthur Rothstein, January 1939.
LC-USF33-003033-M4

Rivers have deeply affected Missouri's land and life. They have long bestowed the benefits of commerce, transportation, and recreation, but they have also demanded to go where they want, when they want. The Mississippi flooded land along most of its length in 1930, 1933, and 1937. Here a photograph shows the numerous wheelbarrows employed by WPA workers on a project to raise the levee in St. Louis.

The RA/FSA was but one of the federal programs aimed at bolstering and reforming the American economy. A 1948 textbook on Missouri government reports, "In our state, roads, streets, parks, airports, water and sewage systems, schools, and libraries were constructed and modernized by the work of the W.P.A. Sewing rooms were conducted for women who had to support families. The articles made in these sewing rooms were given to needy people on relief and to state institutions."[1]

Tearing down buildings, St. Louis, Missouri. John Vachon, May 1940. LC-USF33-001877-M4

Old buildings being torn down, St. Louis, Missouri. John Vachon, May 1940. LC-USF33-001877-M1

The decline of river commerce led to abandoned buildings along the waterfront, many of which were demolished in the 1930s and 1940s. A 1937 Housing Act aimed both to provide jobs and to demolish slums. In St. Louis, clearing the old buildings made way for later construction of offices, hotels, Memorial Parkway (later Interstate 70), and the Jefferson National Memorial Expansion.[2]

Fountain in front of Union Station, St. Louis, Missouri. John Vachon, May 1940. LC-USF33-001903-M2

Milles Fountain across from Union Station was built in 1939. The joining of the main male and female figures in the fountain symbolizes the meeting of the Mississippi and Missouri Rivers.

Interior of old St.
Louis cathedral,
St. Louis, Missouri.
John Vachon, May
1940.
LC-USF33-001876-M4

Grain elevator. Kansas City, Missouri. Arthur Rothstein, November 1939. LC-USF34-029103-D

While we often think of cities as cultural and entertainment hubs, their historic role has been as collection points for goods on their way to market. The photographs of Kansas City predominantly tie the city to the Midwest's farm economy, showing stockyards and grain elevators. These photographs again illustrate the FSA's evolution, as Stryker attempted to keep the Historical Section relevant to a country under the darkening shadow of war. Rather than poverty-stricken farmers, we see America's infrastructure and people who make it function smoothly. As one of the project's photographers said, "We photographed shipyards, steel mills, aircraft plants, oil refineries, and always the happy American worker. The pictures began to look like those from the Soviet Union."[3]

Kansas City, Missouri. General view of part of the stockyards. Jack Delano, March 1943.
LC-USW3-019459-D

Oil tanks. Sikeston, Missouri. John Vachon, November 1940.
LC-USF34-061744-D

Kansas City, Missouri. Hortense W. Thompson, one of several women freight handlers employed at the Atchison, Topeka, and Santa Fe freight depot. Jack Delano, March 1943.
LC-USW3-019729-E

Kansas City, Missouri. Freight rate men at the freight depot. The schedules on their desks list freight rates to various points in the United States. Jack Delano, March 1943. LC-USW3-019403-D

Newton County, Missouri. Camp Crowder area. James Mallory, Ozark farmer whose land has been bought by the Army for construction. With the aid of FSA (Farm Security Administration), he will move to a farm in Bates County one hundred miles north, in the corn belt. John Vachon, February 1942. LC-USF34-064285-D

On the brink of elimination, the politically unpopular resettlement programs of the FSA received one last breath of life in the late 1930s due to the crises created by the sharecroppers' strike and the coming of World War II. Nationally, some fifty thousand people were relocated for the construction of war camps and munitions depots, including Camp Crowder, Missouri, near Springfield. This number does not include the Japanese Americans relocated from the West Coast, some onto land held by the FSA.[4]

The photo opposite is a document of the FSA's success: unlike the barren, eroded, and rocky soil depicted earlier, here we have a healthy harvest on a fertile subsistence farm created for a tiff miner.

Fifteen acre subsistence homestead developed by FSA (Farm Security Administration) for tiff miner Lawrence Corda. Washington County, Missouri. Arthur Rothstein, November 1939. LC-USF34-029120-D

Newton County, Missouri. Camp Crowder area. Construction began in September 1941. Trailer camps, cabins, hotels, liquor stores, cafes, and night clubs stretch along U.S. Highway No. 71 bordering the camp for about ten miles. John Vachon, February 1942. LC-USF34-064226-D

The phenomenal military mobilization for the coming war absorbed much surplus labor, both through recruitment and through the build-up of a civilian workforce. Camps and hotels sprang up to provide living accommodations for Camp Crowder construction workers (photos above and opposite).

By the late 1930s the FSA faced annual budget battles for congressional appropriations. With war looking imminent in Europe, many critics of the New Deal sought to limit Roosevelt's programs by calling for reduction of nonessential spending. By 1941, the FSA had been reduced to a shell of its former self, and in

Newton County, Missouri. Camp Crowder area. Housing for construction workers. John Vachon, February 1942.
LC-USF34-064224-D

late 1942 the Historical Section officially became the Domestic Operations Branch of the Office of War Information (OWI). Although the photographers' new assignment was to support the war effort, the budget battles continued, and in 1943, after eight years as director of the file, Stryker left the FSA/OWI. Among his last acts was to secure the prints and negatives a permanent home in the Library of Congress. With this action he realized his goal of preserving for future generations a photographic record of American life in the 1930s.[5] The FSA itself was replaced in 1946 by the Farmers Home Administration.

At the American Legion booth for collecting scrap paper. Chillicothe, Missouri. John Vachon, January 1942.

LC-USF33-016196-M5

# Chapter 1
## Missouri and the New Deal

1. The precise number of photographs, both in the file and of Missouri, is difficult to determine. Fleischhauer and Brannan report that 88,000 prints have been organized in the file with about 77,000 made under the direction of Roy Stryker. Exact numbers are elusive as these photographs are today housed at the Library of Congress along with photographs and negatives from loosely related agencies, estimated to number 210,000. Carl Fleischhauer and Beverly W. Brannan, eds., *Documenting America 1935–1943,* 333–38. The photographs reproduced here were identified using two sources: the library's Chadwyck-Headley Microfiche collection, and the Library of Congress's website—the Memory Project (http://memory.loc.gov).

2. David Thelen, *Paths of Resistance: Tradition and Democracy in Industrializing Missouri,* xviii.

3. *Official Manual State of Missouri,* 1929–1930, 741, 841–42.

4. Data are drawn from David D. March, *The History of Missouri,* 2:1355.

5. See *Official Manual State of Missouri,* 1935–1936; March, *History of Missouri,* 2:1354–56.

6. Stephen E. Smith, "A Description of Public School Conditions in Missouri during the Depression," 12–16.

7. Franklin Delano Roosevelt, *The Public Papers and Addresses of Franklin D. Roosevelt,* 658.

8. Figures are drawn from March, *History of Missouri,* 2:1370–72; *Official Manual State of Missouri,* 1941–1942, 995–96. Courthouse figures are from Marion M. Ohman, "PWA and WPA Courthouses in Missouri," 95.

9. See March, *History of Missouri,* 2:1367–68.

10. Ibid., 2:1398.

11. Bureau of the Census, *Historical Statistics of the United States, 1789–1945.* Series E 88–104: "General Statistics—Farm Income, Prices Received and Paid, 1910–1945."

12. On the link between farm ownership and the independent yeoman farmers who made up democratic communities, see Sidney Baldwin, *Poverty and Politics: The Rise and Decline of the Farm Security Administration,* chap. 2; Paul Keith Conkin, *Tomorrow a New World: The New Deal Community Program,* 12; and Grant McConnell, *The Decline of Agrarian Democracy.*

Tractor statistics drawn from Louis Cantor, *Prologue to the Protest Movement: The Missouri Sharecropper Roadside Demonstrations of 1939,* 38. Statistics on tenancy in Missouri derived from U.S. Bureau of Foreign and Domestic Commerce, *Statistical Abstract of the United States,* 57th ed. 1935 No. 542—"Number of Farms: By Tenure and by States." On tenancy in Missouri, see College of Agriculture, *Efficient Use of Missouri Lands,* 21. On tenancy and land stewardship, see F. Jack Hurley, *Portrait of a Decade: Roy Stryker and the Development of Documentary Photography in the Thirties,* 18.

13. See John H. Nolen, *Missouri's Swamp and Overflowed Lands and Their Reclamation,* 14–15.

14. The growing of cotton in southeast Missouri is well covered in Thad Snow, *From Missouri.* See also, Cantor, *Prologue to the Protest Movement.*

15. For example, James J. Gosling, *Politics and the American Economy,* 113–15.

16. Christiana M. Campbell, *The Farm Bureau and the New Deal,* 165.

17. Oren Stephens, "FSA Fights for Its Life," 481.

18. On the worthiness of the folks living in different types of poverty, see Baldwin, *Poverty and Politics,* 20–21; later he asserts, "Agricultural lenders came to despise poor and inefficient and small scale farmers" (130). See also Snow, *From Missouri,* chap. 34.

19. Baldwin, *Poverty and Politics,* 84.

20. Quotation from Edwin R. Embree, "Southern Farm Tenancy: The Way out of Its Evils," 153. See Cantor, *Prologue to the Protest Movement,* 11–12, for a discussion of the displacement of the sharecroppers.

21. Donald Holley, *Uncle Sam's Farmers: The New Deal Communities in the Lower Mississippi Valley,* 25, discusses the second New Deal. The RA was created by Executive Order 7027, April 30, 1935; the following discussion is indebted to Baldwin, *Poverty and Politics,* 85–105.

22. Several authors identify the faith in social planning and human progress as a central value in the New Deal programs. Stange links this to John Dewey, taking her book title from a phrase of Dewey's; Maren Stange, *Symbols of Ideal Life.* See also Hurley, *Portrait of a Decade,* 25, and Richard S. Kirkendall, *Social Scientists and Farm Politics in the Age of Roosevelt.* Quotation from United States Department of Labor, "Housing under the Resettlement Administration," 1398. On the Subsistence Homesteads Division, see Conkin, *Tomorrow a New World;* Baldwin, *Poverty and Politics,* chap. 4.

23. Quotation from Collins, "Thirty-three Families Join in Two Co-Operative Farms," 1. Deshee Farms in Indiana was referred to as "Little Russia." See Robert L. Reid, ed., *Back Home Again: Indiana in the Farm Security Administration Photographs, 1935–1943,* 16.

24. Campbell, *Farm Bureau and the New Deal,* nicely traces the evolving role played by the American Farm Bureau Federation in New Deal policies; see also Holley, *Uncle Sam's Farmers,* chap. 13, and 259; and Helen Fuller, "Who Speaks for the Farmers?"

25. Baldwin, *Poverty and Politics,* 201–215; Missouri estimate from Snow, *From Missouri,* 322; tenant purchase program figure from Kirkendall, *Social Scientists and Farm Politics,* 112.

26. The reference is to the title of chapter 9 in Baldwin, *Poverty and Politics.* Holley challenges this view, titling chapter 11 of *Uncle Sam's Farmers* "Disturbers of the Peace? Or Keepers of the Peace?" making the point that the FSA did not go as far as many would have liked.

27. E. Pendleton Herring, "Official Publicity under the New Deal." Statistic on photo-

graphic use from James L. McCamy, *Government Publicity: Its Practice in Public Administration,* found in Hurley, *Portrait of a Decade,* viii. On the difficulty of measuring the size of the file, see note 1.

28. Hurley, *Portrait of a Decade,* ix, presents a slightly different list of three reasons. Two of these, the photographers involved in the project and the sense of history that permeated the RA/FSA, overlap those here. The third, a "commitment to a policy of total truthfulness," is a source of dispute, and will be discussed below. A thorough bibliography of contemporary exhibitions and publications can be found in Penelope Dixon, *Photographers of the Farm Security Administration: An Annotated Bibliography, 1930–1980.* The Soviet Union also had a cadre of talented photographers in the 1930s, but, says Leah Bendavid-Val in *Propaganda and Dreams: Photographing the 1930s in the USSR and the U.S.,* "There was no one like Roy Stryker in the USSR" (54).

29. Quotation from Roy Emerson Stryker and Nancy Wood, *In This Proud Land: America 1935–1943 as Seen in the FSA Photographs,* 7. Press agent quoted in Robert E. Girvin, "Photography as Social Documentation, 219. The emergence of documentary photography in the 1920s and 1930s as a form of communication that depicts reality is discussed at length in Stange, *Symbols of Ideal Life,* and treated in numerous other works, including Bonnie Brennen and Hanno Hardt, eds., *Picturing the Past: Media, History and Photography,* chap. 1. Those who consider the FSA photographers neutral documentarians tend to discuss them in the context of Jacob Riis and Lewis Hines, their famous predecessors. See, for instance, Carolyn Kinder Carr, *Ohio, a Photographic Portrait, 1935–1941: Farm Security Administration Photographs,* 6.

30. Definition from the second college edition of *The American Heritage Dictionary.* Hurley called the photographers' work "propaganda in the best sense" (*Portrait of a Decade,* ix); see also Stryker, *In This Proud Land.* Quotation ("propaganda contrasted") is from Leonard W. Doob and Edward S. Robinson, "Psychology and Propaganda," 88. Other treatments of the file as "good propaganda" include Michael Carlebach and Eugene F. Provenzo, Jr., *Farm Security Administration Photographs of Florida,* who call the efforts propaganda, but in the sense of telling the truth (42); Herbert K. Russell, *A Southern Illinois Album: Farm Security Administration Photographs, 1936–1943,* who agrees that the pictures are "propaganda but not faked" (x); and Beverly W. Brannan and David Horvath, *A Kentucky Album: Farm Security Administration Photographs, 1935–1943,* ix, who note that Stryker and his photographers were propagandizing but that it was good propaganda. But see Strange, *Symbols of Ideal Life.*

31. James Curtis, *Mind's Eye, Mind's Truth: FSA Photography Reconsidered,* reproduces and discusses the several versions of Rothstein's steer skull, as well as the political firestorm they ignited, in chap. 4. In "The Farm Security Administration File: In and out of Focus," F. Jack Hurley debates the issue of ideological motivation on the part of photographers in this "social construction school" (244) of Stange and Curtis.

32. On dignity, see Stryker, *In This Proud Land,* 7; compare Stange, *Symbols of Ideal Life,* 127, for readings of photographs and their presentation that suggest a less dignified interpretation. See Hurley, *Portrait of a Decade,* for the discussion of truth. Part of the difference between the propaganda-as-truth school and the view of propaganda as the tool of larger sinister forces is the weight placed on the autonomy of Stryker and his photographers. For

instance, Hurley, "Farm Security Administration File," makes much of the fact that the individual photographers had various motivations in working for the FSA, a point Hank O'Neal makes clear in discussions with nine of the photographers in *A Vision Shared: A Classic Portrait of America and Its People, 1935–1943*. Stange, on the other hand, presents a thesis about the centralized, top-down planning of the New Deal government, which was embraced by Tugwell when he ran the FSA photographic division. Cultural critics of the FSA photographs also note that the FSA was not killed outright but was changed into the Office of War Information. See Allan M. Winkler, *The Politics of Propaganda: The Office of War Information, 1942–1945*. See Lili Corbus Bezner, *Photography and Politics in America: From the New Deal into the Cold War*, for a discussion of the decline of political photography after the FSA's glory days.

33. Stryker, *In This Proud Land*, 8–9. The earliest academic treatment of these issues I identified was Werner J. Severin's 1959 thesis, "Cameras with a Purpose: Photographic Documentation by the Farm Security Administration, 1935–1942."

34. Baldwin, *Poverty and Politics*, 318 n. 28. On the Farm Bureau in Missouri, see Campbell, *Farm Bureau and the New Deal*, 4.

35. Consistent with the claim that the individual photographs and the entire file are complex and multidimensional, the categories in this book are obviously my creation. Different categories were considered, and some photographs were considered for more than one grouping or chapter.

## Chapter 2
## Environmental and Human Problems

1. *WPA Guide to 1930s Missouri*, 71.

2. Joni L. Kinsey, *Plain Pictures: Images of the American Prairie*, nicely presents varied depictions of the land and human use of it.

3. Jean Douglas Cadle, "'Cropperville'" From Refuge to Community: A Study of Missouri Sharecroppers Who Found an Alternative to the Sharecropper System," 1.

4. Toilet data and quotation from Barrick, "A Study of Housing Conditions of 750 Rural-Rehabilitation Families of the Farm Security Administration," 63, 82. Quotation on coddling from Baldwin, *Poverty and Politics*, 257. There are numerous pictures of privies in the file, both old ones like this, and the new ones that were built by the RA/FSA. Typical of the WPA Federal Art Project's posters promoting sanitary privies is one captioned, "Your home is not complete without a sanitary unit, recommended by the State Department of Public Health" (LC POS-WPA-IL.01.Y67 no. 1). This poster and others can be found on the library's site: http://memory.loc.gov/ammem/wpaposters/wpahome.html.

5. Embree, "Southern Farm Tenancy," 151, distinguishes renters, sharecroppers, and share tenants.

6. Snow, *From Missouri*, 200–23.

7. Union growth and figures from Richard S. Kirkendall, *A History of Missouri: 1919–1953*, 5:193. Strikes by tiff miners and by workers at the Kansas City Ford plant in 1937 are discussed in March, *History of Missouri*, 2:1383.

Chapter 3
Relief and Rehabilitation

1. Snow, *From Missouri,* 179.

2. Information on the CCC and Missouri state parks is drawn from the 1935–1936 and 1939–1940 editions of *Official Manual State of Missouri,* and from information supplied by the Missouri Department of Conservation.

3. Stange, *Symbols of Ideal Life,* 123–27.

4. For a discussion of photographer impression management and subject presentation, see Lawrence W. Levine, "Photography and the History of the American People in the 1930s and 1940s," in *Documenting America, 1935–1943,* ed. Carl Fleischhauer and Beverly Brannan, 20–21.

5. On the evolution of the file, see Hurley, *Portrait of a Decade,* 60. Severin, "Cameras with a Purpose," claims that Stryker shifted focus in part due to a prompting by an editor of *Survey Graphic,* a periodical that used many of the FSA photographs (21).

6. Richard Hellman, "The Farmers Try Group Medicine," 76.

7. Ibid., 72.

8. McCamy, *Government Publicity,* published contemporaneously with the New Deal programs in 1939 gives much credit to the quality produced by the FSA photographers. For an interesting account of the fear of electricity and suspicion of the REA, see National Public Radio, *The Best of NPR: Eyewitness to History,* which includes a segment on the significance of electricity to the lives of many rural residents.

Chapter 4
Radical Reform: Resettlement

1. Lee had worked as an artist prior to taking up the camera for the FSA. "Lee's work is 'straight,' but his point of view is always consciously chosen and actively informed" (Hurley, *Portrait of a Decade,* 12).

2. "The FSA Shows Missouri Its Low-Cost Housing Project," 32.

3. Different types of resettlement projects, including those in suburban areas, are discussed in U.S. Department of Labor, "Housing under the Resettlement Administration."

4. A brief history of the sharecroppers' strike and the subsequent creation of the Delmo Labor Homes Project and their ultimate transference to the Delmo Housing Corporation is found in Steve Mitchell, "'Homeless, Homeless Are We. . . .'"

Chapter 5
Sharecropping: The Stubborn Problem

1. The immigration estimate is drawn from Cadle, who cites Cantor; the Snow quotation appears in *From Missouri,* 145.

2. Whitfield, who was also an organizer of the Southern Farmers Tenant Union, feared

violence and fled to St. Louis. The strike is discussed in Mitchell, "'Homeless, Homeless Are We . . .'"; Cantor, *Prologue to the Protest Movement;* Snow, *From Missouri;* Nicholas Natanson, *The Black Image in the New Deal: The Politics of FSA Photography,* chap. 4; and Candace O'Connor, Steven J. Ross, and Lynn Rubright, "Oh, Freedom after While."

3. "Call a Cropper Probe," 3.

4. See "Evicted Campers on Roads Await Food from State," 1A; "Evicted Farmer Short of Food in Road Camps," 3A; "Evicted Tenants Being Removed from Highways," 1A.

5. On the Delmo Homes, see Mitchell, "'Homeless, Homeless Are We. . . .'" Cadle's thesis on Cropperville is the authoritative source for information on its creation and maintenance.

## Chapter 6
## A Broader Slice of Missouri Life

1. Dominic J. Capeci, Jr., "The Lynching of Cleo Wright: Federal Protection of Constitutional Rights during World War II." Capeci argues that World War II's pitting of the forces of democracy and freedom against totalitarianism induced greater involvement by the federal government in race relations, including the prosecution of some people involved in the 1942 killing of Cleo Wright in Sikeston. See also, Irvin G. Wylie, "Race and Class Conflict on Missouri's Cotton Frontier."

## Chapter 7
## The Cities and the Coming War

1. Quotation from Earl A. Collins and Albert F. Elsea, *Missouri . . . Its People and Its Progress,* 346–47.

2. Kirkendall, *History of Missouri,* 5:19.

3. John Vachon, "Tribute to a Man, an Era, an Art," 99.

4. Stephens, "FSA Fights for Its Life," 485–86.

5. Fleischhauer and Brannan, eds., *Documenting America,* 6–7.

# Works Cited

Baldwin, Sidney. *Poverty and Politics: The Rise and Decline of the Farm Security Administration.* Chapel Hill: University of North Carolina Press, 1968.

Barrick, Bonnie Letsinger. "A Study of Housing Conditions of 750 Rural-Rehabilitation Families of the Farm Security Administration in Missouri." Master's thesis, University of Missouri–Columbia, 1940.

Bendavid-Val, Leah. *Propaganda and Dreams: Photographing the 1930s in the USSR and the U.S.* New York: Edition Stemmele, 1999.

Bezner, Lili Corbus. *Photography and Politics in America: From the New Deal into the Cold War.* Baltimore: Johns Hopkins University Press, 1999.

Brannan, Beverly W., and David Horvath, eds. *A Kentucky Album: Farm Security Administration Photographs, 1935–1943.* Lexington: University Press of Kentucky, 1986.

Brennen, Bonnie, and Hanno Hardt, eds. *Picturing the Past: Media, History and Photography.* Urbana: University of Illinois Press, 1999.

Cadle, Jean Douglas. "'Cropperville' from Refuge to Community: A Study of Missouri Sharecroppers Who Found an Alternative to the Sharecropper System." Master's thesis, University of Missouri–St. Louis, 1993.

"Call a Cropper Probe." *Kansas City Star,* Jan. 12, 1939, p. 3.

Campbell, Christiana M. *The Farm Bureau and the New Deal.* Urbana: University of Illinois Press, 1962.

Cantor, Louis. *Prologue to the Protest Movement: The Missouri Sharecropper Roadside Demonstrations of 1939.* Durham: Duke University Press, 1969.

Capeci, Dominic J., Jr. "The Lynching of Cleo Wright: Federal Protection of Constitutional Rights during World War II." *Journal of American History* 72 (Mar. 1986): 859–87.

Carlebach, Michael, and Eugene F. Provenzo, Jr. *Farm Security Administration Photographs of Florida.* Gainesville: University of Florida Press, 1993.

Carr, Carolyn Kinder. *Ohio, a Photographic Portrait, 1935–1941: Farm Security Administration Photographs.* Akron: Kent State University Press, 1980.

College of Agriculture. *Efficient Use of Missouri Lands.* University of Missouri–Columbia Agricultural Experiment Station, 1935.

Collins, Earl A., and Albert F. Elsea. *Missouri . . . Its People and Its Progress.* Rev. ed. St. Louis: Webster Publishing Company, 1948.

Collins, John M. "Thirty-three families Join in Two Co-operative Farms." *Kansas City Weekly Star* (Apr. 6, 1938): A1.

Conkin, Paul Keith. *Tomorrow a New World: The New Deal Community Program.* New York: Da Capo Press, 1976.

Curtis, James. *Mind's Eye, Mind's Truth: FSA Photography Reconsidered.* Philadelphia: Temple University Press, 1989.

Dixon, Penelope. *Photographers of the Farm Security Administration: An Annotated Bibliography, 1930–1980.* New York: Garland, 1983.

Doob, Leonard W., and Edward S. Robinson. "Psychology and Propaganda." *Annals of the American Academy of Political and Social Science* 178 (May 1935): 88–95.

Embree, Edwin R. "Southern Farm Tenancy: The Way out of Its Evils." *Survey Graphic* 25 (Mar. 1936): 149–53, 190.

"Evicted Campers on Roads Await Food from State." *St. Louis Post-Dispatch,* Jan. 11, 1939, pp. 1A, 7A.

"Evicted Farmers Short of Food in Road Camps." *St. Louis Post-Dispatch,* Jan. 12, 1939, p. 3A.

"Evicted Tenants Being Removed from Highways." *St. Louis Post-Dispatch,* Jan. 14, 1939, pp. 1A, 2A.

"The FSA Shows Missouri Its Low-Cost Housing Project." *Business Week* (Apr. 8, 1939): 32.

Fleischhauer, Carl, and Beverly Brannan, eds. *Documenting America, 1935–1943.* Berkeley: University of California Press, 1988.

Fuller, Helen. "Who Speaks for the Farmers?" *New Republic* 106 (Feb. 23, 1942): 267–68.

Girvin, Robert E. "Photography as Social Documentation," *Journalism Quarterly* 24 (Sept. 1947): 207–20.

Gosling, James J. *Politics and the American Economy.* New York: Longman, 2000.

Hellman, Richard. "The Farmers Try Group Medicine." *Harpers* 189 (Dec. 1940): 72–80.

Herring, E. Pendleton. "Official Publicity under the New Deal." *Annals of the American Academy of Political and Social Science* 179 (May 1935): 167–75.

Holley, Donald. *Uncle Sam's Farmers: The New Deal Communities in the Lower Mississippi Valley.* Urbana: University of Illinois Press, 1975.

"Housing under the Resettlement Administration." *Monthly Labor Review* 44 (May 1937): 1387–1400.

Hurley, F. Jack. *Portrait of a Decade: Roy Stryker and the Development of Documentary Photography in the Thirties.* Baton Rouge: Louisiana State University Press, 1974.

———. "The Farm Security Administration File: In and out of Focus." *History of Photography* 17 (autumn 1993): 244–52.

Kinsey, Joni L. *Plain Pictures: Images of the American Prairie.* Washington, D.C.: Smithsonian Institution Press, 1996.

Kirkendall, Richard S. *A History of Missouri: 1919 to 1953.* Vol. 5. Columbia: University of Missouri Press, 1986.

———. *Social Scientists and Farm Politics in the Age of Roosevelt.* Columbia: University of Missouri Press, 1966.

Levine, Lawrence W. "Photography and the History of the American People in the 1930s and 1940s." In *Documenting America, 1935–1943,* edited by Carl Fleischhauer and Beverly Brannan. Berkeley: University of California Press, 1988.

McCamy, James L. *Government Publicity: Its Practice in Public Administration.* Chicago: University of Chicago Press, 1939.

McConnell, Grant. *The Decline of Agrarian Democracy.* Berkeley: University of California Press, 1953.

March, David. *The History of Missouri.* Vol. 2. New York: Lewis Historical Publishing, 1967.

Mitchell, Steve. "'Homeless, Homeless Are We. . . .'" *Preservation Issues* 3, 1 (1993): 1, 9–12.

Natanson, Nicholas. *The Black Image in the New Deal: The Politics of FSA Photography.* Knoxville: University of Tennessee Press, 1992.

National Public Radio. *The Best of NPR: Eyewitness to History.* New York: Time Warner Audio Books, 1997.

Nolen, John H. *Missouri's Swamp and Overflowed Lands and Their Reclamation.* Jefferson City: Hugh Stevens Printing, 1913.

O'Connor, Candace, Steven J. Ross, and Lynn Rubright, producers. *Oh Freedom after While.* San Francisco: California Newsreel, 1999. Videotape.

*Official Manual State of Missouri.* Jefferson City: Botz-Hugh Stephens Press, 1929–1930.

*Official Manual State of Missouri.* Jefferson City: Midland Printing, 1935–1936/ 1939–1940.

*Official Manual State of Missouri.* Jefferson City: Mid State Printing, 1941–1942.

Ohman, Marion M. "PWA and WPA Courthouses in Missouri," *Missouri Historical Review* 96 (Jan. 2002): 93–118.

O'Neal, Hank. *A Vision Shared: A Classic Portrait of America and Its People, 1935–1943.* New York: St. Martin's Press, 1976.

Reid, Robert L., ed. *Back Home Again: Indiana in the Farm Security Administration Photographs, 1935–1943.* Bloomington: Indiana University Press, 1987.

Roosevelt, Franklin Delano. *The Public Papers and Addresses of Franklin D. Roosevelt.* Vol. 1. New York: Random House, 1938–1950.

Russell, Herbert K. *A Southern Illinois Album: Farm Security Administration Photographs, 1936–1943.* Carbondale: Southern Illinois University Press, 1990.

Severin, Werner J. "Cameras with a Purpose: Photographic Documentation by the Farm Security Administration, *1935–1942*." Master's thesis, University of Missouri–Columbia, 1959.

Smith, Stephen E. "A Description of Public School Conditions in Missouri during the Depression." Ph.D. diss., University of Missouri–Columbia, 1934.

Snow, Thad. *From Missouri.* Boston: Houghton Mifflin, 1954.

Stange, Maren. *Symbols of Ideal Life.* New York: Cambridge University Press, 1989.

Stephens, Oren. "FSA Fights for Its Life." *Harpers* 192 (Apr. 1943): 479–87.

Stott, William. *Documentary Expression and Thirties America.* New York: Oxford University Press, 1973.

Stryker, Roy Emerson, and Nancy Wood. *In This Proud Land: America 1935–1943 as Seen in the FSA Photographs.* Greenwich: New York Graphic Society, 1973.

Thelen, David. *Paths of Resistance: Tradition and Democracy in Industrializing Missouri.* Columbia: University of Missouri Press, 1991.

U.S. Bureau of Foreign and Domestic Commerce. *Statistical Abstract of the United States.* 57th ed. Washington, D.C.: Government Printing Office, 1935.

U.S. Bureau of the Census. *Census of Partial Employment, Unemployment, and Occupations: 1937.* Vol. 3. Washington, D.C.: Government Printing Office.

U.S. Bureau of the Census. *Historical Statistics of the United States, 1789–1945.* Washington, D.C.: Government Printing Office, 1949.

U.S. Department of Labor. "Housing under the Resettlement Administration." *Monthly Labor Review* 44 (June 1937): 1387–1400.

Vachon, John. "Tribute to a Man, an Era, an Art." *Harpers* 222 (Sept. 1973): 96–99.

Winkler, Allan M. *The Politics of Propaganda: The Office of War Information, 1942–1945.* New Haven: Yale University Press, 1978.

*WPA Guide to 1930s Missouri.* Lawrence: University Press of Kansas, 1986. Originally published as *A Guide to the "Show Me" State.* St. Louis: Duell, Sloan and Pearce, 1941.

Wylie, Irvin G. "Race and Class Conflict on Missouri's Cotton Frontier." *Journal of Southern History* 20 (May 1954): 183–96.

*Index*